THE POWER OF PERSONAL EQUITY

Simple Steps to Recession-Proof Your Business or Career

JOE OCCHIOGROSSO

Become The Author You Always
Wanted Or Needed To Be...

Published by

MENTOR Equity
PRESS

www.Mentor Equity Press.com

www.ThePowerOfPersonalEquity.com

The Power of Personal Equity
Simple Steps to Recession-Proof Your Business or Career
Joe Occhiogrosso

Published by Mentor Equity Press, International
New York

Mentor Equity Press, Intl. is exclusively owned and operated by
Success Connection Team, Corp.
www.MentorEquityPress.com

Cover Design, Interior Design and Layout by Parry Design Studio, Inc.

Printed in the United States of America

First Printing – September 2011

ISBN: 978-0-615-53876-1

TABLE OF CONTENTS

TABLE OF CONTENTS

DEDICATION

To all my family and friends that make each day so fulfilling.

"Most people are more afraid of success than failure. Deep down we all know our potential is limitless and this makes many individuals uncomfortable. They stop when they feel they are growing too much or too fast and may become something too special – and that's a real shame. We were all put here to become as special as possible. This book is to reassure you that you can have it all. You deserve it all. Anything less is being disrespectful to your Maker."

—Joe Occhiogrosso

ACKNOWLEDGEMENTS

Just a few years ago, I never would have believed that I'd become a published author. I recall struggling to pass my required Expository Writing class as a freshman at Rutgers University back in 1983. As I matured and decided to tackle my weaknesses, my writing greatly improved over the years. My parents, Claire and Frank Occhiogrosso, had been mentioning over the last few years that I should consider writing a book. I owe so much to my parents for always making me feel I was special and could achieve anything I set my mind to. Thanks, Mom and Dad!

My wife Annmarie is truly a special person. She's one of the kindest and most loving people you will ever meet. I can't imagine my life without her. Being married to a serial entrepreneur with a hyper-social personality can be challenging for any woman—but Annmarie just lets me do my thing. She has given me great support with any new venture I've taken on. Whether it's starting a new career or writing a book, she has never doubted my capabilities and potential to make things work. It's her blind faith in me that has made me so successful. Love you with all my heart, honey!

My three wonderful kids—Alex, Stephanie, and Frankie—remind me every day of what life is all about. I can see so much of Annmarie and me in them. I'm very proud that they're growing up to be such loving and caring young adults.

I'd also like to thank my brother John for being such a great friend and godfather to my three children. I'm blessed to have many close friends—most of whom I've known for decades. They make my life fulfilling and a lot of fun: Frank and Susan Marone, Mike and Michelle Marotte, Bart and Michelle Oates, Bill and Bridget Trochiano, Stephen and Trish Lemanski, Angelo and Rose Bagnara, Martha and James Caponigro, Francesca and Paul Venino, Bob and Pennie Quintana, David and Leslie Konikow, John LoPresto, Anthony and Robin Piccolo, Brett and Joan Glenn, Rob and Andrea Alexander, Dr. George and Robin Mitilenes, Patrick and Suzie McGeough, Joseph and Kathy Timko, Ray and Trish Abbiatici, Jay Helverson, Jim Morris and Dory Devlin, Peter Heiden (who left us way too early), Chris Brasco, David Nixon, Dr. John Tumillo, Sal and Maryann Burdi, Steve and Christine Reilly, Bill Dwyer, and Dr. Bill Quain, to name just a few. Thank you all for your friendship and support.

I'd like to also acknowledge some truly talented and gifted people I've met through the Viridian network and other business/friendship ventures: Michael Fallquist, Rob McFadden, Bob Ulrich, Cami Boehme, Roop Bhullar, Meredith Berkich, Glen and DeAnn Crawford, Charles and Amanda Costello, Bob Meneve, Joel Brizzi, Ashley Nolan, Tom Klaas, Brenden Kenny, Ed Kenny, Jim Kenny, Mike Moore, Bob Gaydos, James Leonhardt, George Schiaffino, Michael Fitzpatrick, Henri Aymonier, Michael and Debbie Masiero, Bob Florentine, Pat Giglio, Steve Finch, Larry Hopkins, Ron Tortu, Scott and Melissa Epstein, Terry Walker, Jenna Marzulo, Bobby DeChiaro, Alison Bradford, Anthony Robbins, Scott Friedman, Annie Liu, Ted Terhune, Lynn Danzker, Herb Palmer, Steve Barrios, Heidi Simon, Scott Bloom, Jeff Shelton, Patrick Lull, John Zoller, Ed and Gail McGuiness, Cathy O'Mealia, Anthony Busciglio, Justin Woolf, Marc Marsi, Mike and Justin DiMedio, Steve Finch, Big Bo Bowidowicz, Big John Payonteck, Bobby Cerchione, Scott Fletcher, Glen Stevens, Pat Welsh, Brett Marcus, Dan Swiniarski, Tom Cioffe, Jimmy and Kym Boucher, Phil Doblosky, and Kevin Gillen. My sincere apologies if I've left anyone out.

And lastly, I thank my publisher Mentor Equity Press International (Marc Grant) for being so persuasive and encouraging me to take on this project.

FOREWORD

Here is a book for "the rest of us"—the millions of ordinary men and women who are normal, hard-working people. We pay our bills and take care of our families. We don't want advice from celebrities, nor do we relate to stories about people who were in prison or on drugs. We go to church, send our children to decent schools, and dream of a better life!

We need a book with real-life, common-sense, simple solutions. Joe O's book is just what we need. With straightforward language and excellent examples, Joe takes us on a journey of success. And, to make it even better, Joe uses fantastic stories of everyday people—just like the rest of us—who "made it big" by following a few, time-tested principles.

Joe O. isn't a homeless person who pulled himself out of the gutter to create his fortune. Nor is he the son of rich parents who set him up in business. He is one of us—an ordinary person. Yet, he reached deep into his imagination to create an innovative strategy for success. And because he did, ordinary men and women can duplicate his practical, easy-to-understand, motivating formula for achieving the very best that life has to offer. With just two words—Personal Equity—Joe defines the ultimate key for your personal breakthrough. No tricks, no magic, just a step-by-step plan that anyone can master. Best of all, we have Joe's example to follow. Joe did the hard work. Now all we have to do is follow in his footsteps.

Joe says, "You can't inherit Personal Equity, and you surely can't buy it—yet it can be the most valuable asset you ever own."

This is great news for "the rest of us". With these words, Joe fills us with hope. How many times have we been shut out, kept off the insiders' list, or held back from our full potential because of the high cost of entry? Folks, Personal Equity is the most democratic of assets. It costs nothing to develop. It is blind to race, gender, and financial situation. If you don't have Personal Equity right now—no problem! You can start creating it in the next moment—and Joe shows you how.

Consider his three steps for creating Personal Equity:

Follow through - for you

Expect to score

Create your future in the now

Do you see anything here about investing money? Does Joe say, "If you're born with special talents, or to the right people, you can do this."? NO! In fact, Joe is the son of a policeman and a legal secretary. If you needed special circumstances to succeed with Personal Equity, someone else would have written this book.

If you are serious about making significant changes in your life—changes that will bring you wealth, stress-free living, and meaningful relationships with other successful people—then this is the book you have been waiting for. But to get all the rewards you deserve from this book, you need to follow the first step that Joe lays down.

You need to follow through—for you.

You need to follow through on the promise you made to yourself when you bought this book. Did you know that the average person only reads 11 pages of a personal-growth book? Isn't that sad? No one buys a book thinking, "I will only read 11 pages." They think, "I'll bet the answers I am looking for are right inside these pages."

Well folks, the answers you are looking for are right inside these pages. So make this book count for you, by learning to count on yourself. Follow through—for you!

Personally, I found this book to be absolutely riveting. I literally could not put it down. Joe doesn't just give you facts and theories. He weaves great stories throughout the book. My favorite? No doubt about it, Second-Cousin Vito. But, that story is way in the back of the book, and I want you to promise me one thing—don't read it until you have read the chapters in front of it. Cousin Vito has a lot to teach all of us —but we need some basic information to make his story most effective.

Finally, I can't end this foreword without recommending Joe's last metaphor. Become a flower, and become a diamond. Take my word for it, you want to do this.

If you are going to commit to one tool this month, make it this book. Go ahead, get started. And as you read these pages, you will soon realize that you are not ending at the last page—you are just getting started.

Thanks Joe! "The rest of us" appreciate it.

Bill Quain, Ph.D. Best-selling author of 19 books with more than 2.3 million copies sold including his latest book *Happy Leap Year.*

Employ your time in improving yourself by other men's writings, so that you shall gain easily what others have labored hard for.
—Socrates

INTRODUCTION

W hat makes certain people more successful than others? Is it what they do on a consistent basis? Is it the result of learned behavior and consciously adopted beliefs? Or were they born knowing how to be successful, with a core-level belief in themselves?

I do think some people are more inclined toward success than others, perhaps because they're innately competitive and had good role models and influences early in life. However, I believe everyone can achieve success with the right mindset and skills—and these can be developed. The fact that you're reading this book shows you already have the first element of that mindset—the intention to succeed.

HOW DO I DEFINE TRUE SUCCESS?

My definition of true success changes slightly from time to time—and yours may too. However, my core definition includes having certain benefits of life I think we all would enjoy: an abundance of free time, plenty of money, fulfilling relationships, and the vibrant health to enjoy it all. *The Power of Personal Equity* focuses on ways to achieve the first three by freeing up your time and greatly enhancing your wealth, while connecting in mutually beneficial ways with like-minded people.

Most people can't figure out the secret to achieving this kind of success, which is why less than 1% of Americans can retire comfortably before the age of 50. However, success can be achieved quite simply if you understand and use the ideas I suggest in this book, based on my own experience and that of many others.

WHAT IS PERSONAL EQUITY (PE)?

First, let me explain what Personal Equity, or what I often refer to as PE, is not. It has nothing to do with your net worth. It's not about your investment portfolio, the home you live in, or the car you drive. Your personal equity is not a tangible item that can be valued on paper or traded online, and it's not your assets minus your liabilities. Nor is it about your formal education or what people think and say about you. (Their opinions—good or bad—aren't relevant because you know you're on the right path.) You can't inherit PE, and you surely can't buy it—*yet it can be the most valuable asset you ever own.*

So what is Personal Equity? PE is a form of personal and professional "enlightenment," which you can start developing today and enhance over time. Your level of PE can be measured by how well you incorporate certain principles as well as standards into your business and personal dealings. As you use these principles and embody high standards, you not only raise your PE, but you increase your business success and wealth as a natural result. When you achieve a high level of PE, you're truly successful by any definition because you're not out to rise above everyone else, but to bring as many people up with you as possible.

Again, the benefits of personal equity include more free time, increased income, and more fulfilling relationships. Plus, you'll have the joy and satisfaction of knowing you've helped fellow travelers in the journey of life along the way.

Whether you're seeking success in the corporate world or as an independent business owner, I invite you to discover the secrets to building personal equity I reveal in these pages. When you put them to use, you may find it's never too late—or too early—to have a happy retirement. Unless, of course, you're having too much fun to fully retire.

Money is neither my god nor my devil. It is a form of energy that tends to make us more of who we already are, whether it's greedy or loving.

—Dan Millman

CHAPTER 1

LEARNING A UNIVERSAL LAW

C an you have high Personal Equity if you work for a large corporation? Certainly. Jack Welch has sky-high PE, and he worked for General Electric for many years. No doubt his PE helped him become the chairman and CEO. So yes, you can, but it's quite difficult to reap that degree of benefit from your PE working for someone else. Besides, you have a better chance of becoming an All-Star Major League Baseball player than you do of becoming a legendary CEO.

What's the best way to truly recession-proof your career and gain the money, free time, and fulfilling relationships that result from high PE?

OWN a business. Develop a client base, a following that's truly *yours*. Can you achieve this working for a large institution? Perhaps. But only on a limited basis and with no *legal* ownership. To me, that's way too risky. There's nothing like having actual equity on paper. If you're already entrenched in corporate America with a thriving career, good—but I advise you to work on Plan B at all times. The purpose of this book is to inspire you to act when a propitious time and opportunity arise. To this end, I tell my personal story.

Mine is not a tale of rags to riches. I was never homeless, nor was I ever in drug rehab or prison. However, in some ways my success is even more remarkable considering I grew up in a blue-collar, middle-class family. Why is that? When you're down and out and have nothing to lose, you have lots of incentive to go for it. On the other hand, when you grow up working class, you tend to be conservative and play it safe. *Don't dream too big*. Being ultra-successful or "enlightened" isn't part of your parents' or teachers' consciousness or the local neighborhood work ethic. Even your peers can hold you back. I was lucky that my parents always supported me and gave me the confidence that I could do whatever I wanted to do in life —and fortunately I believed them because oftentimes children don't believe their parents.

For whatever reason, though, I always strove to build my Personal Equity, even before I coined the term—improving my social skills, my listening skills, and my physical body, and just making friends. When I was young, the concept of using Personal Equity to build your own company and reap the highest benefits was foreign to me because my career path seemed clear.

Why I Started Out on Wall Street

My dad was a detective with the New York Police Department (NYPD) and had always been interested in the stock market. He'd seen a few childhood friends no smarter than he was start out as low-level clerks on Wall Street and become quite successful. (By Wall Street, I mean financial services firms located in New York City.) These Wall Street guys drove beautiful cars and had big homes, and some even enjoyed expense accounts. My parents wanted me to enjoy this upper-middle-class lifestyle too, so they had a plan for me to attend college. Most of these people who started out in the 1960s had barely graduated from high school, but by the 1980s, a college degree had become almost a necessity to "get on the Street." By the time I needed to choose a major in college, I was also on board with getting on the Street since I noticed that my friends whose dads worked there enjoyed the finer things in life. (Back then, moms didn't have executive jobs on Wall Street, at least none from my neighborhood.) These families were the first to get VCRs and microwave ovens; they went out to dinner more often; and some of my friends even got brand new cars when they turned 17.

Most middle-class kids growing up on Staten Island, New York pursued one of two career paths. One was to graduate from high school and take the written test for a City job, which basically meant as either a policeman, firefighter, or sanitation worker. The other route consisted of college and a job on the Street. I was groomed for option two, which suited me just fine. It seemed I would do well downtown because I was good with numbers and had the gift of gab.

I graduated from Rutgers University at age 20 with a BA in Economics and a B+ average, and people like me were in high demand at the time. This was back in 1987 before the stock market crashed in October of that year. Financial firms were riding high through most of the 1980s and hiring people every day. Wall Street recruiters invaded my campus in New Brunswick, New Jersey, pleading for us to come to New York City for an interview. In the spring of my senior year, I had at least 15 interviews with major investment banks boasting exciting and prestigious names such as Goldman Sachs and Citibank. Anyone with fairly good grades from a decent school was hired that year. *"Can you can start the Monday after graduation?"*

MY BUBBLE BURSTS

So the interviews and job offers flowed in—*but with a catch*; all of these jobs were "back office" positions for the operations department. In the 1980s, firms still needed a lot of clerks to process and clear the thousands of daily trades. At the time, pay for these positions ranged from about $21,000 to $23,000 a year, with two weeks of vacation, other benefits, and a 401k retirement plan. Yes, a retirement plan. Whoopee. That was the last thing I was excited about at age 20.

Back office operations? What would someone like me do in operations except sit there bored and miserable? I wanted to be on the trading floor, yelling and screaming, or at least in the mergers and acquisitions department, where the big money and action were. However, that fantasy was dispelled during the first few interviews that spring of 1987. I discovered that unless you had a close relative with a lot of influence, these high-profile jobs were offered only to candidates with a master's degree, specifically from a great school. When I inquired about these more exciting departments, my interviewers tried not to laugh. *Here's a kid with an undergraduate degree from a state school—and no connections.* They advised me to create a five-year plan. Start out in the back office, and after two full years of loyal work, they would offer to pay for my master's degree! At the time, tuition to grad school amounted to more than my annual salary, so it sounded like a great opportunity—at first.

But here came another catch. I would still be working full time and would have to pursue my degree *at night and on weekends.* Ugh! That was the best plan they had for me? Start studying for the entrance exams (GMATs), try to get into a part-time MBA program at a local university such as NYU or Columbia, and get my MBA at night? After working nine to ten hours a day, I'd go sit in a classroom across town and get home at 10 p.m. to start my homework. At 23 years old, I'd be looking at three to four years of pure hell. What about a social life? What about staying fit? NO! My life would consist of working then studying and attending classes on all my nights and weekends! Nights and weekends—heck—what else do young people in their 20s live for?

Although I had a lot of interviews and job offers, you can see why I wasn't excited. In fact, I was rather depressed about the whole darn thing. As I write this book, the unemployment rate in the U.S. is the highest it's been in decades. So most people would probably say, "At least you had some job offers. Most recent college grads today can't find any work." I wish I'd known back then *not to worry* about my future. I wish I'd had a book like this to learn from. I wish I'd known about Personal Equity.

A BREAK—OR WAS IT?

Back to the job offers. It started to sink in that my life would be tough for the foreseeable future, but I was becoming comfortable with the fact that if I really wanted to make it big on Wall Street, I had to pay my dues. A free MBA at age 26 wouldn't be so bad, would it? I knew my life would suck for a long while, but at least I was on my way.

With two or three similar offers on the table from a few reputable firms not far from the train and Staten Island Ferry, I almost didn't go to the last interview I'd scheduled with Shearson Lehman Brothers. The mom of one of my younger brother's friends worked as an executive assistant there. (Isn't that how most people get their first job?) She passed my résumé on to the HR department and was very excited and proud when I got a call for an interview because she was far from a big shot at the firm. However, I wasn't looking forward to it because I'd already narrowed down my choice to two firms I felt had more name recognition. I also knew it would be the same old story: start in operations and work your way up the ladder. I almost cancelled, but I couldn't let my supporter down. So I put on my $99 suit and hauled myself up to the 101st floor of the World Trade Center.

I'm not exactly sure why this particular interview turned out to be different from all the others, but for one thing, I wasn't at all nervous the way I had been on my first few interviews. I was completely relaxed, knowing I had pending offers and also knowing what to expect. In fact, before the HR woman even got into it, I let her know I knew the drill and wasn't really interested in the "start in the back office and kill yourself for five to seven years" plan. However—I told her—it seemed to be the only thing out there for someone like me, and I was probably going to do it anyway. So unless Shearson Lehman offered me $24,000 a year (an extra $1,000 a year more than the other firms), I wasn't interested. Imagine that! I was letting an extra $1,000 a year—less than $14 a week after taxes—greatly influence my entire career decision-making process. Crazy, wasn't it? But a lot of people operate like this.

After about 10 minutes, she pulled out a file and said something like, "I do have this one particular opening on the foreign exchange trading desk." Then she added that it took a certain type of personality to work on that floor, and I might be well suited for it. I immediately perked up. Trading desk? Tell me more. I wasn't sure what "foreign exchange" meant, but that didn't matter. "Positions Clerk is the title," she said—not glorious at all, almost beneath someone with a college degree from a decent school. A lot of yelling, screaming, and even occasional swearing goes on. I'd basically be a "go-fer," doing everything from getting people coffee to writing their trading tickets and making sure their positions balanced out every night. The biggest responsibility would be ensuring that no trades were missed so the firm wasn't at any unknown financial risk overnight. Other than that, just basic math and keeping cool under pressure. Now *this* sounded interesting!

She scheduled an interview the next week with the "Chief Dealer." What the heck is a Chief Dealer? I didn't ask, but I found out soon enough that the chief dealer is basically the boss of the trading desk. This particular guy was about 30 years old, and he was in charge. I walked onto the 7th floor of the American Express Tower (at the time Amex owned Shearson Lehman) and into his office. He immediately reached for a roll of Tums as he told me to have a seat. He informed me that, basically, the Positions Clerk job was a no-brainer. It involved simple math. I wouldn't be utilizing any of the stuff I'd learned in my 300-level advanced microeconomics/calculus class that had kept me up at night. He also told me the eight or ten people on "the desk" were all in their mid 20s and early 30s and making over six figures a year. Most of them had started out in this very position I was seeking.

I would have to report every day at 6:45 a.m. and stay until the work was done. No lunch break at all. I would eat my free lunch at my desk when I had the chance. A quiet day would end at 6:30 p.m., but if a crisis arose or new economic data was released, I had to stay late. How late? As late as it took… maybe 8 p.m., maybe midnight. I couldn't leave until I had entered all the trading tickets correctly and matched up all the positions. Salary? The job would pay $18,000 a year, and because it was technically a "management" position, it didn't pay overtime.

This deal amounted to about 20 percent less than my best offer. It paid $346 a week! With a typical 60-hour work week, that figured out to be $5.76 an hour. I was making more working part-time as a security guard at the Staten Island Mall. A lot of my friends would think I'd lost my mind working for such low pay. Well, I guess I always had the entrepreneurial spirit, rolling the dice and sacrificing short term gain for a big-time future.

The chief dealer asked if I was interested in this position. Absolutely! I lived at home rent free, and if there was ever a time to take a chance, it was now. This could be my ticket to a big salary without having to get my MBA.

But he didn't offer me the job just yet. Another candidate wanted the position, and not only was she the daughter of a senior vice president at Shearson, she had interned in the very same position in their London office the previous summer. It wasn't looking good. I recall asking the question rather directly to challenge the "chief": "So do you have to hire this daughter of the SVP?" He assured me he was the boss and would hire anyone he wanted. I gambled a little there, but it definitely helped because a week later he offered me the position. I accepted over the phone on a Thursday and showed up on Monday morning, the first of June, 1987.

In fact, I began work immediately after my last final exam—two full weeks before I even walked down the aisle to receive my diploma. I'm not sure what the rush was for me. I guess I couldn't wait to get to work for corporate America. Today, I would consider that a fate worse than death! No one could possibly pay me enough to work for a big company with an hour-plus commute.

During my college years, getting a job on Wall Street had been my dream career and main focus. I "knew" it was actually going to happen, just as my parents and I had planned. Although I wasn't aware of it at the time, I learned a valuable lesson: *If you want something badly enough and really focus on it, it will become a reality.* I didn't know this was a universal law, an actual fact of life. Heck, I thought I just got lucky. Now I know better.

THE GAMBLE PAYS OFF

The first day passed in a blur as I met people and started my training in the foreign exchange (FX) business. The second day, June 2, 1987, legendary Fed Chairman Paul Volcker announced his retirement and the desk went crazy. I watched helplessly as people screamed and yelled: "I need a price on $20 versus the Yen!"… "I need to buy 50 million deutschmarks *now!*" I had no clue what any of this meant.

I distinctly recall taking home some trading tickets as samples to review with my dad that night. We weren't exactly sure if they were trading $20 or $20,000,000 because no one took the time to fill in all the zeroes. Surely the latter, no? Yes. I figured it out the next day. Thank goodness I didn't ask anyone because it would have been embarrassing. FX desks trade billions every hour. That fact I wasn't sure after my first few days strikes me as highly comical in hindsight. The good news: I was now involved on a big-time trading desk.

Not only did this gamble to take a lower-paying job in exchange for a ride on the fast-track pay off for me in the long term, it actually paid off in the short term too. When the stock market crashed just five months later in October 1987, huge layoffs came down across the board. New entry-level back-office people were among the first to be let go. However, the foreign exchange markets only got busier during the late 1980s, and with a salary barely above minimum wage, I was never in jeopardy of losing my job.

I will never forget Black Monday, the day the stock market crashed on October 19, 1987. The U.S. dollar was collapsing, and we were so busy that day I didn't even bother to go home that night. I wasn't going to be done tallying up the trades until after midnight anyway, and the night desk was also trading so my morning work was piling up before my eyes. I slept for an hour or so on a leather couch and started again at 5 a.m.

I fit in well on the Street. A good student of the game, I quickly realized that street smarts and an engaging personality *after* work at dinner or cocktail hour were almost as important as one's trading abilities.

FX traders were highly specialized. With fewer than 200 of them in the entire U.S., they collectively traded well over a trillion dollars a day. So once they had a few years experience, they were generally set for a long while. FX trading was extremely profitable, and all banks, large and small, wanted to either have a presence or growing presence. In addition to all the large U.S. banks and investment houses, almost every single bank in

Europe and Asia had a New York branch so they could trade efficiently in the 24-hour FX market.

I moved up the ladder fast and began trading my own "book" after six months, but I felt I wasn't getting the respect I deserved. After all, a mere six months earlier I had been fetching coffee. So I stayed at Shearson Lehman for only one year. I quickly leveraged my connections on the Street, interviewed at a rival bank, got the job, and more than doubled my salary. It was the right move.

I ended up working for three different investment banks in my first three years. Why? Well back then, we foreign exchange dealers were in great demand. The equities markets were in a lull after the crash of 1987, but FX trading was very profitable. As I was out two to three nights a week networking and building my own early version of Personal Equity, I became more and more popular and in demand. We were all free agents, and the offers kept rolling in to make a move for more money and more responsibility.

I was learning that what I really wanted and focused on I could get— and my PE helped me get there.

Throw back the little ones, and pan-fry the big ones.
Use tact, poise, and reason, and gently squeeze them

—*Steely Dan*

CHAPTER 2

IF YOU WANT TO GO FISHING, PICK A BIG POND

My trading experience gave me ample opportunity to build my PE and discover what I *could* do—and it also helped me realize what I *wanted* to do and *didn't* want to do, where I wanted to be and didn't want to be.

The more I traded, getting my bank's name out there, the more PE I created in the FX market. I had moved from Shearson Lehman and, at age 22, I was now the junior deutschmark (DM) trader at one of the largest trading banks in the U.S. The name of the bank was Security Pacific National Bank (Sec Pac), a behemoth on the West Coast and a direct rival of Bank of America—until they merged in 1992. Little known by the average person on the East Coast, the bank had an all-star New York FX trading desk at the time. I was fortunate to be on the fast-track, assisting the Chief Dealer and some of the senior dealers on the deutschmark desk.

One magical Monday when we were going to be short-staffed for the week, the Chief Dealer informed everyone during our 7 a.m. meeting that "Joe will be our deutschmark trader this week." So there I was, having finished my senior year at Rutgers just two years before, with my only worry in the world being which party to attend, now sitting in one of the most prestigious trading seats in the FX business.

THE KNOW-LIKE-TRUST FACTOR

We had only two ways to trade FX currencies back then—either directly with other banks over the Reuters Dealing Machine (the equivalent of today's Instant Messaging) or through the live-spot FX brokerage firms. These five or six different FX brokerage firms competed for the FX dealers' attention and support. I learned early on that people prefer to work with those they know, like, and trust. And what better way to get to know someone than to socialize after hours? I was good at that.

Entertaining was a huge part of the FX culture back in the day. With millions of dollars being traded every few seconds and daily brokerage fees of $2,000 to as much as $5,000 a day per trader rolling in to these firms, dinner and drinks were always available. (Besides business contacts, I also made a bunch of life-long friends while networking. In fact, this is how I initially met my current business partner Frank Marone. He and his cousin Anthony Piccolo were FX brokers and we are still close friends today.) If my bank was paying their firms $50,000+ a month, offering me an expensive dinner and a limo home was no big deal. Because I was young and single with no children and worked at a big-name bank, I enjoyed an evening out about two to three times a week. Dinner and drinks at whatever Zagat's claimed to be the hottest restaurant and a limo home? Twist my arm!

I wanted to meet as many people as possible, so I was never in a big rush to go home and watch television. Somehow I innately understood I needed to build my PE and knew how to do it. In addition to allowing my brokers to complete their entertainment quotas for the week, I happened to be a fun "date". I could talk shop, politics, or sports. Many of my brokers had barely graduated from high school, so they often asked me to join them and help them out when they were stuck with some Ivy League genius who wanted to discuss the Elliot Wave Theory of market analysis. I was more than willing to tag along and learn from someone smarter and more experienced than I was. It was yet another way to build my PE—all while eating at NYC's trendiest restaurants. I even had a chance to meet a slew of celebrities. I made it a point to politely shake hands with as many famous people as possible. People like Madonna, Woody Allen, Robert De Niro, and Eddie Murphy to Rudy Giuliani and Henry Kissinger, just to name a few.

So there I was, a young hired gun, trading the most influential currencies—U.S. dollars and German deutschmarks—for one of the most prestigious New York trading banks. We happened to have huge customers out of Malaysia who liked how quickly and fairly we provided two-way pricing for their $100 million deals. The typical market trade at the time was $5 million or $10 million. So when I needed to quote a price on $100 million, I needed to do it quickly and use my gut to instantly figure out if this was a buyer or seller. One bad quote could kill my entire week. In addition, even if I quoted it properly, I had to liquidate my position as efficiently (and hopefully as profitably) as possible.

All the banks in the FX market in both the U.S. and abroad would see the "Sec Pac New York" name either selling or buying U.S. dollars and pushing the market—at least for the next two to three minutes, and maybe for the rest of the day. Seasoned dealers throughout the market would ask their spot broker, "Who is this guy throwing this volume around and making me sweat?"… "It's Joe O. from Sec Pac. You met him at the 21 Club a few months back, remember? The kid with all those funny stories." I even had people from London and Frankfurt asking me to dinner when they were in town.

Now was I some kind of wunderkind? Did I, at age 23, have the FX markets all figured out? Not even close. In fact, I didn't make much profit, if any. My job was to hold down the fort, not get slaughtered, and keep the clients happy for Sec Pac while they searched for a senior trader. The head office in Los Angeles knew I was on the DM team, but I don't think they knew I was on my own and doing all the trading. I was determined to make the most of the opportunity and make it difficult for them to move me off the hot seat. I didn't know if I would be the lead deutschmark dealer for one week or one month, but I steadily built my PE.

REPLACED—BUT NOT FOR LONG

I tried to live day to day and not be concerned that Sec Pac was actively interviewing for a seasoned and experienced trader. The mighty Sec Pac couldn't have this kid who wasn't even an officer and was making a mere $35,000 a year be their lead trader for long. The position back in 1989 paid about $250,000 plus bonuses and perks. So obviously I was a real bargain. With each pay period, the bank saved a bundle of money and added to its bottom line.

After a few weeks, I showed them I could handle the job and assured them that with a little more experience I could be dynamite in the very near future. Why couldn't they just keep me in the hot seat forever? Why spend $250K a year for the devil you don't know? I pleaded with them to just pay me a salary of $75K and we'd all be happy. However, the brass out in Los Angeles couldn't justify it. *What if this kid loses a huge chunk of money one day? Eleven months ago, he was writing trading tickets and making coffee—and now we're going to more than double his salary and make him an officer?* As they say in New York, "Ain't gonna happen."

So after about two months of me being the toast of the town and having a great time throwing billions of dollars around, they hired a "real" professional trader. My job was to sit next to him and support and learn from him. A diamond in the rough, I would be polished by his wisdom and become a great asset to the bank.

This particular FX trader had been sitting at home when they hired him. Supposedly, he'd just come off a monster year and taken home a $3 million bonus. He'd had exchanged tough words with his old management team, so he "retired." In his early 30s, of course he wanted back in after a few months. Being good friends with one of our senior traders, he interviewed and got the job.

My manager sat me down and told me what a great opportunity this was for me, making it seem as if I'd be working with some trading genius like Warren Buffet. I took it all in stride and was determined to make the best of the situation.

As it turned out, Mr. Legend was gone in a week. We had a wild and crazy moving market one day, and right in the middle of a large deal, he collapsed at the desk. It was one of the scariest moments I'd ever experienced. There he lay, convulsing on the floor and bleeding from his head from the fall, as the market was moving and we were losing $10,000 every few seconds. People were screaming and yelling to help him and also trying to cover the trades. News had come out that an oil tanker in the Middle East had been bombed, and our senior trader happened to be holding the wrong position. In addition, all our clients were panicking and wanting to get out of their positions too.

My new buddy and mentor lay on the floor dying, with five people trying to help him, and I was told to "just cover the position and get out of it!" So I had to trade my way out of this mess. It was ugly. We lost over $600,000 in under 10 minutes. If he hadn't collapsed, it would've been a fraction of that amount.

The new guy was raced to the hospital, and he recovered in a few days. I never knew for sure what happened, but it seemed like a panic attack. Many people told me later that he had a substance abuse problem and was seriously unhealthy. They said he'd stay out all night partying and drive straight to work. He'd drink ten cups of coffee during the morning and smoke incessantly at the desk right next to me. (Smoking wasn't allowed even back in 1989, but he did it anyway.)

They had to let him go, so good old Joe O. was back in the saddle again as they interviewed for another senior trader. Meanwhile I was thinking… *I'm a good, young, coachable kid. Why not give me a shot? I'm cheap and adequate.* … Wasn't gonna happen. So I realized I had to move on. My PE had risen greatly in the previous six months, so once I put the word out, I had more than a few offers.

PE TO THE RESCUE—AGAIN

On my 24th birthday, I took a position of senior deutschmark dealer at a major French bank in New York with a base salary of $90,000 plus bonus. It was a good situation for the bank because that was cheap for a trader, and it was a *big* raise for me. Within four years, my salary had increased 500 percent. I now had serious income for 1990—heck, even for today. My only real expense was my share of the rent, which was only $325 a month at the time, so I had plenty of spending money. My new salary came to three times what any of my friends were making—even the really smart ones who went to great schools. Did I get this new job offer only because I was such a great trader? No, I was still quite green at the time. I got it because my Personal Equity was off the charts high for such a young guy. I was well-liked, sincere, and trustworthy. I was a good listener and a hard worker.

So what's the lesson here? *Always* be working on and growing your Personal Equity. It's all you can depend on. Sec Pac didn't care about me and my future; while I was there, two of my bosses who promised to "watch my back" left for other jobs. So I couldn't be complacent. I could've been apprehensive and traded defensively while I sat in the hot seat. I could've been the type of person to go straight home and never say yes to any dinner or social event. But that would have been risky. Way too risky for me. By this time, I could clearly see the value of consciously building my PE.

DISASTER BRINGS ME UP SHORT

My new position at the French bank didn't last long—less than a year, actually—and then I was fired. Yes, Joe O. was fired. I was trading for about nine months and doing pretty well, but I happened to be short $17 million during a certain moment in time on the morning of Aug 2, 1990, when we received the news flash: "Iraq Invades Kuwait." A war had broken out while I was short dollars. *Not good.* In times of panic, people bought U.S. dollars for safety and security. Especially in the Middle East because the world needs U.S. dollars to buy oil, and if production ceases and prices skyrocket, the dollar is in high demand. Hence the absolute dollar-buying frenzy that ensued. It took me about five to six minutes to cover the position and buy my dollars back, but I lost over $350,000, which was almost everything I had made for the year. All that hard work and my profits were gone in an instant. The bank didn't fire me because of what happened. The managers knew a lot of people lost big that day and such an event was part of the FX life. However, I couldn't get over it. The market's erratic behavior for the next few months exposed my inexperience. I was extremely gun-shy and tentative and had a pit in my stomach every day. My will to improve and build my PE all vanished.

Ironically, just two minutes before that news broke, I had a long position of about $6 million. If the news had come out two minutes earlier when I happened to have the "lucky" position, I wouldn't have lost $350K. Instead, I probably would've made $100K and may still have been there today. Who knows? That's the crazy thing about life.

So once they called me in and said, "It's not working out," I couldn't really argue with them. In fact, I was kind of relieved. I did learn that my boss liked me a lot and the French banks take good care of their people—even when they let them go. Despite the fact I had less than one year of service, the bank granted me six weeks of severance pay. Plus, because my rent was low and my FX broker friends had helped pay for most of my nightlife and entertaining, I'd saved up a good portion of my salary. I needed a mental break, and I wanted to take two to three months off and re-think my whole FX path.

THE OTHER SIDE OF THE STREET

When word got out that I was let go, I received a barrage of phone calls at home. I wasn't in the mood to talk that day, so I didn't answer the phone and was in no rush to call anyone back. But one FX broker friend of mine kept calling and asking that I return his call ASAP. I didn't want to rehash the whole story or hear him try to cheer me up, but after he called three times, I thought I owed him a call back. I figured he was worried about me so I should let him know I was okay. When I called, however, he wanted to relay a message from his boss that their firm wanted to hire me immediately! Why? Because of my high PE, of course.

I was shocked and a bit surprised at first that they would offer. Although it wasn't all that unusual for an FX trader to make the career change to "the other side" and become a broker, I'd never considered it myself. Trading was much more prestigious. As educated bankers, traders had to decipher world economic news instantly and manage millions of dollars of risk. FX brokers, on the other hand, were deemed middle men. They didn't care if the value of the dollar went up or down because as long as they were booking transactions, they'd get paid. Switching from trader to broker was a step down in the FX world. It was an admission that you couldn't handle the trading side.

As I thought about this opportunity, my first inclination was: "No thank you, not for me. I'm a highly trained trader and this would be a step down." However, the thought of not having to try to figure out the market every minute of every day did appeal to me. After all, I'd given my heart and soul for the last six months of trading, only to see all my profits vanish in seconds. Maybe I shouldn't leave my future up to chance. I knew a lot of traders by then, and I could certainly relate to their lifestyle. These traders would now be my potential clients and would love to work with a former trader because I'd walked many miles in their shoes. In addition, I was a lot of fun to be around and would be ideal for entertaining the clientele.

Still only 24 years old, I was being offered a base salary of $120,000 plus bonus, a hefty expense account, and a company car. A few other trading offers came in the next week, but I felt that the FX broker side of the business was the right move for me. I thought it meant the stress of my trading and speculating days was over—but little did I know, it had only just begun.

The FX brokers were also quite active in the spot markets, getting stuck with out-trades and errors and having to trade their way out of them. They provided liquidity for the market, despite the fact they weren't supposed to. The brokers did this well however, and the entire market greatly appreciated it even though no one discussed it openly.

I had a great five-plus year run as an FX broker. I kept getting raises and bigger bonuses, and I traveled all over Europe first class. My last year, I was promoted to run the entire spot Japanese Yen desk. It was a big honor for a 29 year old to "run a desk," and I was up for the challenge. Here was my chance to make a million dollars a year. The desk wasn't profitable when I took it over, and if I could turn it around, I'd be in charge of all the bonuses. The firm made it clear that I could take as big a bonus as I wanted. It would never be questioned.

So I had finally arrived. I'd built my PE sky high in the FX world and was being rewarded for it. But, my sphere of influence remained limited. Unless I was in a room full of currency traders trading currencies for a major international institution, I couldn't expand my client base. My client-building activities were limited to a very small circle.

CHANGE BECOMES RAMPANT

Within a year, banks started merging regularly. JP Morgan, Chase Manhattan Bank, Chemical Bank, and Manufacturers Hanover were each significant clients, and they soon all became one bank! Others did the same. Then technology began to burgeon. Online trading platforms rendered the spot FX brokers and direct phone lines inefficient—almost obsolete. And finally, even the currencies merged! Instead of deutschmarks, Swiss francs, French francs, Italian lira and others, we now had the euro. Major consolidations took place on both the trading and brokering sides.

My last year in foreign exchange, I worked twice as hard and made half the money, so I decided I had to move on. I still have many wonderful friends who survived the consolidations, and some are doing better than ever. However, I no longer had the passion. At 30 years old, I had a great reputation and a world of invaluable experience in a market that had all but vanished. I was like a typewriter repairman.

I'd built huge PE in non-residual businesses for other peoples' companies in a limited niche. In other words, I'd spent a lot of time fishing in a small pond that was drying up. Never again. I needed to re-invent myself and find a bigger pond.

As you become more clear about who you really are, you'll be better able to decide what is best for you—the first time around.
—Oprah Winfrey

CHAPTER 3

BUILD YOUR PE
WITH A FEW BASICS

I've always been one for constant expansion, for ongoing improvement and growth. But look around you. How many people merely "exist" compared to those who enjoy an ever-increasing Personal Equity? Astronomers tell us the universe is continually expanding—and we also have this capability. Then why do so few people get what they want out of life? The answer is they don't know how to create it. This chapter addresses several critical factors in this process that will help put you on the fast track to building your PE: follow through, expect to score, and create your future in the Now. So let's get started.

FOLLOW THROUGH—FOR YOU!

Many people lack the basic skill of following through. They tend to get excited and take on a project or develop an action plan then quit before it's accomplished. It happens all day, every day. People let themselves down.

How many Americans join fitness centers during the first week of January? The treadmills and stationary bikes that sat idle in November and December have a waiting list in January. By the first week of February, the crowd thins out and the flow becomes a trickle again. The regulars who are committed to a healthy, steady fitness program just shake their heads as they watch ninety-five percent of the people give up on their New Year's resolution. Only about five percent stick with it, get in shape, and stay in shape, making a real life change—and I'll bet five percent is high.

Whether it's a fitness goal or life plan commitment, people in general tend to lose focus and quit. They often don't realize that if only they would follow through on the little things, the big things would come. Success is incremental.

ARE YOU IN THE NINETY-FIVE PERCENT OR THE FIVE PERCENT CATEGORY?

No doubt you have good friends and colleagues who always follow through for you. They go to great lengths to show up on time and deliver as promised. If they say they'll bake a cake and be there by 8 p.m., you can count on it. Or if they say they will have a report finished and on your desk by the morning, it's always done. Following through with others is an admirable virtue, to be sure—but how many of these people go to great lengths to make sure others deem them reliable but consistently break promises to themselves?

Think of the most reliable people you know—people who are always there for you, who would drive at midnight through a rainstorm to pick you up—but who aren't there for themselves. They let themselves down time and time again. It's often something small, such as planning to take a brisk walk in the morning and then deciding to skip it and stay in bed. Or perhaps buying a book and never getting past the first chapter.

Here's the dilemma: Once we start letting ourselves down on a consistent basis, it becomes the norm. We think it's acceptable. After all, we're not harming anyone else, right? Or are we? Maybe we're not as healthy or prosperous as we should be and our family suffers because of it. But we don't think of that because it's tough to measure.

If you're like most people, you feel it's more important that *others* not speak ill of you so you hide your personal weaknesses. If this sounds like you, be aware that this behavior becomes a vicious cycle with serious consequences. You begin to expect failure. It defines you to yourself. Your journey to improve *you* must start with delivering on a consistent basis for *you*. Otherwise you won't trust yourself. You will make pacts with yourself, all the while knowing it's okay to default.

Remember, your Personal Equity doesn't stand for just your reputation; it stands for you. Are you content with where you are today? Do you make excuses and rationalize, not taking certain actions because you have no one to answer to? Of course, like everyone else, you have good days and bad days and take the easy way out once in a while. But start limiting these times and following through more often, and see what happens to your PE.

> *"The mind is a superb instrument if used rightly. Used wrongly, however, it becomes very destructive. To put it more accurately, it is not so much that you use your mind wrongly — you usually don't use it at all. It uses you. This is the disease. You believe that you are your mind. This is the delusion. The instrument has taken you over."*
> —Eckhart Tolle

Now am I telling you anything you don't know? Of course not. My role here is to inspire you to start making small, consistent changes in the way you think and function that can have a *huge* impact, both short and long term.

EXPECT TO SCORE

One of the changes you can make that will result in a huge difference is to raise your expectations.

Consider Jerry Rice, the Hall of Fame wide receiver who's scored more touchdowns than any other NFL player in history. Rice was obviously a highly gifted athlete, but the League is full of gifted athletes. In fact, Jerry Rice wasn't the fastest or strongest on his team—but he was the best. Why were faster and stronger players on the bench (or waiting tables back home) while Rice became a legend? Expectation made all the difference. (I love using sports as an analogy because it shows that we're so much more than physical beings.)

I heard about Rice's secret of success from my close personal friend and business partner, Bart Oates, who played on the same team as Jerry Rice when he won a Super Bowl with the San Francisco 49ers. A three-time Super Bowl Champion himself, Bart went to law school in the off-season and later became a super successful entrepreneur.

Jerry was already a living legend when Bart played with him, and he was still the hardest working player on the team. When he practiced catching drills with all the other receivers, he sprinted into the end zone to simulate a touchdown after every catch, regardless of where the drill was being run on the field. *He expected to score every time he caught the ball.* Here was perhaps the best player to ever play the game—his own teammates in awe of him—catching the ball and running full speed, sometimes 60 or 70 yards, into the end zone with every drill.

So if you're a rookie or another starting wide receiver on the team, what do you do? Do you also catch the ball and sprint full speed into the end zone in the August heat like Jerry Rice? The coaches aren't asking you to do this. All you really need to do is learn the routes, catch the ball, and get back in line. You have another three to five hours of drills left in the day. Do you begrudgingly sprint to the end zone to support your legendary teammate—or just to fit in and not look bad?

When you see someone get the results *you* want, yes, absolutely do exactly what they do. But for *yourself.* Why has Jerry Rice scored more touchdowns than any other player in NFL history? Maybe because his mind and body have been trained to score touchdowns and don't know anything else. If you had the opportunity to be on the line in a drill with Jerry Rice, not only would it serve you to also "score" every time, but buy in 100 percent to the reason he does it. If traded to another team, keep on doing it. Be a leader on that new team with a proven drill that works and don't worry that your new teammates may think you're a show off or trying to make them look lazy.

What would happen if you practiced this "expect to score" attitude with *whatever* you're working on—whether you're envisioning a big sale or getting your kids to do their homework?

I incorporated this attitude when I became involved with the Viridian Network in 2010. After a few months of production, I received an official email that said something like, "Congratulations! You earned $13,500 for last month." I took the email and doctored it up a little, adding a zero to the end, moving a comma, and changing the date to read six months in the future. I then forwarded the email to myself and copied my business partner, Frank Marone. I did it as a playful goal-setting drill to make that kind of money seem more real and attainable. And guess what—it worked!—almost to the penny. I should have added *two* zeros!

> *"Mindset*
> *+ Skillset*
> *+ Execution*
> *= Peak Performance"*
> —*Bob Quintana*

What's the principle behind positive expectation, or acting as if something is already true? The mind doesn't know the difference between reality and fantasy. It only knows what it experiences. Your dreams at night seem so real because they are real to your mind. That's why your heart races and your rate of breathing increases during a stressful dream. So use this fact of nature to your advantage. Convince your mind that you've already achieved success. Convince it that scoring a "touchdown" isn't a once-in-a-while, if-I-get-lucky, occasional event, but something that's fully expected and you're quite used to achieving. Let it become the norm.

This technique is especially helpful for people who are *not* comfortable with success. Some people have issues, or negative beliefs, about making a lot of money or becoming too popular, and they sabotage their own progress, often without even knowing they're doing it. I find this unfortunate. We weren't created to hold ourselves back but to maximize everything we've been given and to grow each day.

So if you have thoughts and beliefs that are keeping you from fulfilling your potential, work on changing them so you can freely give your gifts to the world and fully enjoy the rewards.

PUTTING MYSELF OUT ON A LIMB

Now if simply running 60 yards into the end zone each and every time will make me a better player, I'm in. I used this technique well before I was even aware of its value—before I knew it was based on a universal law that works every time. I took full advantage of this type of drill—naively and not too wisely at first, but it worked. Here's what happened.

To conquer oneself is a greater victory than to conquer thousands in a battle.
—The Dalai Lama

I moved out of my parents' house at age 23, which was not a popular move with my parents at the time. However, my new job was in midtown Manhattan, and my commute from Staten Island was insufferable. Although I barely had enough money to pay the rent and car payment and eat, I did have a credit card with a $10,000 line. Did I stay at home on weekends and save money? Did I live within my means and only go out once a weekend instead of three times? Did I refrain from eating out, buying rounds of drinks for my friends, and taking vacations? Heck no! Why didn't I? Because I knew in my bones that there was no real risk in running up my credit card. I fully expected my salary to triple and quadruple and to also receive big bonuses. I felt that any sign of holding back would demonstrate to myself that I didn't truly believe in my destiny.

Now was this a good plan based on fact? Or was it just a way for a 23-year-old kid to justify his over-spending ways? In retrospect, of course, I see this was more than reckless. Anything could have happened to my fast-track career. My bank could have merged at any time, and I could have been laid off while I was $10K in debt. Oh, I did feel I was special and had great things coming (as should *you!*), but who knows what the future holds?

So please understand, I am NOT advising you to overextend yourself and go into debt. I've learned a lot since then, and living with little to no stress is the key for you now. When you have high PE, you understand the balance between pushing yourself to higher things and minimizing undue stress. Back then, I "knew" I was unstoppable. Deep in my soul, I somehow felt I was *already making* millions of dollars. And then it started to happen. The cash, the promotions, and the bonuses started rolling in. The financial aspect of my PE rose like a rocket.

Again, please don't misinterpret what I'm conveying here. I'm just sharing my own real-life experiences, and they turned out well. I ran up some serious credit card debt, had a good time, and then paid it all off nine months later with my first big bonus. I often wonder, though, what might have happened if I hadn't moved out on my own and taken on this lifestyle; if I had bitten the bullet and put up with the long commute every day and saved money living at home. Would I have been that much more ahead of the game financially after I received that first bonus? I don't know for sure. Probably not; because some self-doubt might have crept into my subconscious, and I may not have followed through with such conviction.

I had set a universal law in motion without knowing what I was doing. In fact, I had it down cold. As I said, I *knew* and *felt* deep in my soul, body, and mind that I was already successful. I didn't know enough about the "real" world to doubt. When you have that kind of conviction, the universe supports you full tilt. But not everyone has it naturally, and not everyone was brought up in a supportive environment like I was. Most people have to build this kind of conviction—but *you can do it*. And let me tell you: Committing to yourself at a high level truly does work. When you do, the universal law brings you what you need to fulfill that conviction and commitment.

If you want to take advantage of this expectation technique, I warn you to please be very cautious about debt. When I did this, I was young and reckless and didn't fully understand debt and all its evils. However, I'd like to suggest something just as powerful: *Make your goals public.* When you come up with a venture or project you want to take on, be sure to let everyone know where you'll be in six months or one year and have them hold you to it. This will build your accountability and put your expectations of yourself into high gear, which will activate universal law in your favor.

CREATE YOUR FUTURE IN THE NOW

If you had unlimited amounts of Personal Equity right now, what would you do with it? Would you work from home or nearby, knowing you can come and go as you please? What would it feel like to be making more money than you can spend? I'm not talking about being comfortable; I'm talking about not having to work ever again. Whether you're 25 or 75, if you make the most of your opportunities, you get to decide what you want to do.

> *What we can or cannot do, what we consider possible or impossible, is rarely a function of our true capability. It is more likely a function of our beliefs about who we are.*
> —*Tony Robbins*

So what would you be doing? Sounds like a tough question, right? Well, if you have an abundance of Personal Equity, it wouldn't be a tough question at all because you would know. The answers would be clear and feel right. Why? Because you would already be doing what you were born to do.

Remember how I defined "enlightened" in the introduction? To me, it means incorporating into your personal and professional life the principles and standards I'm presenting in this book. If you simply focus on increasing your PE, you will become enlightened, and the right career choice will appear. It will be self-evident. For example, if you're a business executive in a Fortune 500 company, you may be guided by your inner knowing to quit and start your own consulting company and set your own hours.

This concept of feeling that you already have something you want is similar to living in the present moment. One of my favorite books is _The Power of Now_ by Eckhart Tolle. I highly recommend it if you want to know how to live and create from "the Now." It's both a blessing and a curse that humans can reason and think. Why is it a curse? Because our minds can take over our lives with meaningless and negative thoughts that pull us out of the Now, where we are peaceful, happy, and creative.

We need to find quiet time and still our mind so we can fully know that we are all part of nature and the universe, and we are all omnipotent. Our limitations are self-imposed.

Tolle's book explains how to deeply appreciate the moment but is clear this isn't a skill you need to work on; it's something you can do right now. You can put the book down at any time and get to that still point of knowing. It may be fleeting, and your mind may wander, but the realization that the ongoing chatter in your brain is *not* who you are gives you a taste of living in the Now. You may experience this knowingness and peace for only a few seconds, but it will grow if you keep stilling your mind.

Your Personal Equity can be just as fleeting. If you don't have much yet, or you don't have as much as you desire, the important thing is to see and feel the benefits of having it. Then your experience will keep expanding in your mind until it becomes your physical reality.

What would you do if you had all the money and time you could ever want? Would you like to inspire others? Feed the poor? Help sick people in third world countries get the medicine they need? Help fund a cure for diseases? Take a vacation in Tahiti? Buy a yacht?

Have some fun with this and make it work for you. Visualize *now*, in your present moment, what you want to create in your life. If you can do something physically to help yourself "get there," do it: Go to an open house at your dream home. Test drive a Maserati GT Turisimo. Whatever it is, see it, smell it, touch it, taste it, feel it in your bones. Make it part of your present reality in your mind. Just as I knew at a deep level that my future was guaranteed (even though I had no verified fact to base this on), create that feeling in yourself that what you want is already a reality, no matter what—and it will be.

Follow through for *you*, expect to score, and visualize your own "touchdown." Whatever outcomes you choose can be the fruits of your PE quest.

I enjoyed high school and college, and I think I learned a lot,
but that was not really my focus.
My focus was on trying to figure out what businesses to start.
—Steve Case

CHAPTER 4

THE BIRTH OF PLAN B

I started out with a decent foundation in life. I'd been successful in school, and I had good friends and harmonious family relationships. I always showed up when I promised, and my friends knew they could rely on me. At work, I delivered with the same conviction, which helped me get ahead during my first five years on Wall Street. I kept moving up the corporate ladder about as fast as possible. By age 24, I was already a vice president at a major financial institution, making well over $100K a year. But it wasn't until the winter of 1992–93 that I took my life to a whole new level. I vividly recall that turning point.

MY DISCOVERY

One of my FX broker colleagues, who sat right next to me, started acting and speaking differently. He had much more conviction now than he had before when he closed trades, and he took charge when necessary. Within a short span of time, he seemed to transition from just "one of the guys" to one of the leaders. Before I had a chance to mention what several of us had noticed, he brought up the subject of "personal development." He shared with me a program he'd recently completed. It was the Anthony Robbins's 30-day cassette program from late-night TV. My first reaction echoed that of many at the time: "C'mon—really? That giant rah-rah guy at 2 a.m.? Isn't he just another charlatan selling dreams?" But my colleague convinced me to give the program a try. I couldn't argue with the positive changes I'd seen in him firsthand.

Right away, we discussed truly committing to follow through and not miss even one day. Remember what I said in Chapter 3 about following through? Here was my test. The program included five one-hour tapes a week for four weeks in a row. No excuses. In fact, he played me just right. He didn't just dump 20 hours of tapes on me all at once; he gave me one a day. He could easily do this because I sat right next to him. He would let me have the next tape only if I'd listened to the previous night's tape, and I had no reason to lie. Who would I be kidding if I did that? And of course because we traded all day long on the Street together, we would never lie to each other anyway (although for some reason it seemed okay to exaggerate the results of the weekend's golf game). The 30 days flew by, and only a few times did I find it truly inconvenient to listen, but I budgeted my time and got it done.

Those who know me now, probably think that following through and listening to all 20 tapes in order five days a week for four weeks in a row wouldn't be a big deal for Joe O. He's a high PE guy and he always follows through. However, this wasn't the case 20 years ago. I consistently followed through for others, but not always for me. With the program, though, I didn't find it that difficult to do because I found the material so interesting. It opened up a fascinating and expansive new world for me.

At the time, I didn't know anything about structured personal growth programs and didn't know it was a science. I had never even heard of the *Think and Grow Rich* guru, Napoleon Hill, or the countless success stories out there. I guess I assumed that people such as Henry Ford and Thomas Edison were just smart and lucky. I didn't know they were also deep thinkers, constantly searching for what it takes to succeed.

So the Robbins program was a huge turning point for me. It made me think in an entirely different way. I began to realize I had a lot more to learn about "peak performance." On Wall Street, I was surrounded by all types of talented people—some who had Ivy League educations, some who'd barely graduated from high school, and others in between. The ones who were thriving had figured out aspects of life they hadn't learned in college or on the streets. They had a handle on the "mental game." The Robbins technology showed me that even ordinary people can achieve extraordinary things if they have a mental game plan.

I remember thinking during those first 30 days of the tapes that probably a large percentage of the people who paid full price for the series never finished it. I was fully determined *not* to be among them. Heck, I got the tapes for *free*, and I still finished every single one. I guess the timing was right for me; I was ready to take my life up a notch.

During that first month, I began each day feeling great. I was in a better mood and more thoughtful and respectful to family, friends, and strangers. I recall feeling like I was unstoppable—that not only could I achieve great things for myself and my family, but for others too. The program had given me grand ideas about life, and I had determined where I wanted to be in five years and 10 years. Best of all, it opened my eyes to start working on my Plan B. I was newly married, and my wife and I planned on having a family soon. Did I want to keep working these super stressful 60 to 80-hour weeks? I had lots of grumpy colleagues in their mid and late 30s who weren't healthy or happy. Would that be me in 10 years? Besides, what good is having children if you can't spend quality time with them? My colleagues with children never saw them in the morning because they had to leave before 6 a.m. Oftentimes, they wouldn't get home until 7:30 or 8 p.m., just as the toddlers were going to sleep.

I knew a few people who took less stressful and lower-paying jobs within the trading field, but then their spouses had to work and they had to hire a nanny. My wife, Annemarie and I didn't want to settle for this.

We both grew up with a mom at home and wanted our kids to have that luxury. The Robbins program allowed us to see that we could have it all.

The program led me to become an Anthony Robbins junkie, reading all his books and listening to all his tapes over and over again. It's amazing to me how many people buy self-help books or business career books and never read more than a chapter or two. Again, it's about following through. I can see not finishing a novel if you don't find it entertaining. However, you can always learn something from an educational book. You might discover only one small technique, but it could change your life. You may miss it the first time through, so read your coaching books more than once. Have you ever watched a movie again and realized how much you missed the first time? I've watched *Forrest Gump* many times for example, and I always pick up another good message.

Becoming a Robbins fan also involved attending many of his seminars. I once participated in an event where we learned a mental technique that allowed us to walk barefoot on hot coals without being burned!

So I got to meet Tony Robbins in person. I've seen him a few times over the years, and I explained to him in detail what he'd done for me. I'm surely not the only one who gives him this feedback, but I still wanted to tell him.

Not only did I benefit from Tony himself, but through him, I gained another guide on my journey. At one of the first Robbins events I attended, I noticed my old friend Bob Quintana in the front row. I knew Bob from the local gym during my college days, and we reconnected. He had partnered with Robbins and had become Tony's most successful independent trainer and coach.

I asked Bob how and why he'd gotten so involved with Robbins. He told me he thought the best way to enhance his personal growth was to not only master the technology but teach it. Wow . . . now that's commitment!

Reconnecting with Bob Q. became instrumental in my endeavors to grow my Personal Equity because he had copious amounts of it, and I began attending his local seminars in the 1990s. I gained not only a terrific friend but a true mentor. Since then, Bob and I have teamed up to help thousands of people with Network Marketing.

When you do big things with great people, you will see big and great results. Surround yourself with these types of people and watch your life change for the better. (Thanks, Bob Q.!)

GETTING MY TOES WET WITH NETWORK MARKETING

Shortly after my introduction to the personal growth phenomenon, I was approached to attend a Primerica Financial Services meeting. I loved the idea of starting a part-time business career that would pay me residuals. If you're not familiar with the concept of residuals, it means I would continue to be paid on an initial sale every time one of my customers paid (in this case) the insurance premium. In addition, if I brought people into the organization, I received a percentage of their sales. It was a traditional network marketing company. Besides the residuals, I loved helping people with their financial issues and protecting their families with life insurance when appropriate. This business opportunity would allow me to keep working full time as a trader while I explored my plan B.

I attended a few meetings, signed up as a representative, and soon got my life insurance license and made a few sales. But I was still a slave to my trading desk, my one-hour commute to the suburbs, and my career. I didn't have the time or energy to build a solid side business. However, I'm eternally grateful for that Primerica experience because it planted a seed in my mind about residual income and the benefits of starting my own business—any business. I learned a lot about tax write-offs and other secrets of the wealth builders and also gained a newfound respect for the industry. I finally understood the concept of leverage and helping others while helping myself. To me, it made a ton of sense.

About 15 years later, I was ready and decided to try Network Marketing again. This was one of the best decisions in my career. My experience in Network Marketing has become one of the most challenging and rewarding journeys I've ever taken in my life.

Network Marketing may well be the most misunderstood marketing channel of all time. People who have no clue how it works may dismiss it as a "pyramid scheme," which is pure ignorance. It also gets a bad rap because so many thousands of people have lost their few hundred bucks start-up money—and their self-esteem—failing at it. However, most of these failures were due to a lack of training. Solid Network Marketing companies conduct serious business and should be taken seriously by anyone who wants serious results.

Everyone needs at least some training when starting anything new. Take any Fortune 500 CEO and stick him or her behind a cash register at a fast-food restaurant during a busy time of day with no training at all, and he/she will fail. Even though running a cash register isn't difficult, without at least 15–30 minutes of learning where the buttons are and how to operate it, the results would be disastrous.

"No one ever fails in a good Network Marketing business, they just quit before they reach their goals"
—*Frank Marone*

Me? I'm always open-minded about any business model that's been proven, and I've grown to love trainings. I was aware that this could work exceptionally well for people who knew what they were doing, and I had tremendous respect for anyone who was successful at it. I have to admit, though, I was a little hesitant at first because of the stigma. It's often more socially acceptable to say I'm a Wall Street trader or a traditional local business owner than to tell people I'm involved in a direct selling or network marketing business. But I wasn't bothered as much by the stigma or by using the model as a way to make a living as I was by the way I thought people might react to me. I now know these silly comfort zones of "fitting in" come with a price—and sometimes a steep one.

Now that I've become one of the most successful network marketers in the world and enjoy a lifestyle beyond most people's dreams, I don't care what people think or say. Lesson here? I shouldn't have worried before either. I teach that people with high Personal Equity never need to worry about what others might think as long as they go with their gut. But we're all human, and even leaders like me falter from time to time. I have to stay on my toes and make sure I practice what I preach.

WHY HAS IT TAKEN SO LONG
FOR NETWORK MARKETING TO GET APPROVAL?

All new and great ideas go through several stages. At first they're laughed at and deemed ridiculous. Then they're vehemently opposed, and eventually they're accepted as the obvious truth. Take the idea of the world being round. For thousands of years, most people thought the world was flat. It certainly looked flat, and to say it was round seemed ridiculous. Then thoughts arose over the centuries that it may indeed be round… "Maybe it's just really big and we can't see that it's round."… "Well, the moon is round, and surely the moon would seem flat to an ant crawling along its surface."… People got upset at this notion, though, and the mere mention of it was vehemently opposed… "Don't say it's round! We don't want to deal with such a big change."… And then, of course, when the earth was proven to be round, the idea was finally accepted as the obvious truth.

An example in business is the department store concept. For hundreds of years, local merchants sold one or two specific items. When you needed shoes, you bought them from the shoemaker. You likely received great personal service, and perhaps the shoemaker custom made your shoes within a few days or weeks. If you needed a new dress, you'd go to the dressmaker; for a new hammer and some nails, the local hardware shop.

Then, in the late 1800s, along came Frank Winfield Woolworth, who came up with a new idea for the distribution of goods. He combined all the products and services of these local merchants into one big store with different departments and called it a "department store."

Crazy!!! You weren't going to get that customized service; you were going to have to pick out your shoes and try them on yourself. That seemed a bit ridiculous. And how could anyone buy a dress that was already made? It would never fit!

Well, the department store concept started to take off, and then it went from being called ridiculous to being vehemently opposed. The merchants got together and tried to pass legislation declaring the department store idea illegal. Illegal? How and why was this illegal? That's how angry people were. However, any sharp businessperson could see it wouldn't be deemed illegal for long, if indeed it ever could be. Why? Because it was working! People were getting what they needed at better prices, and Woolworth was making money, too. You might call this concept free enterprise, evolution, or ingenuity. How could this be a bad thing?

As you know, Woolworth's became one of the greatest stories in U.S. history. In fact, the Woolworth empire grew so big so fast that in 1910, Frank Woolworth commissioned the construction of the tallest building in the world to be built in downtown New York City. No construction loans for him; he paid 100 percent in cash. It was finished in 1913 and remained the tallest building in the world until the Empire State Building took the title in the 1930s.

NETWORK MARKETING SUCCESS

Network Marketing, or Relationship Marketing, as it's sometimes called, is thriving now more than ever. It's simply a distribution channel—a way to get a product or service to the people who want to buy it. The most productive network marketers make the most money, just like any other business model. They sell more than their compatriots and bring in more marketers under them to do the same. If they're selling a decent product or service and the system is sound, it's a win-win-win.

For example, my good friend Scott Fletcher has built himself a highly successful career with Primerica Financial Services and has helped thousands of others build their own organizations. I knew him only casually at first. When I found out what he did for a living (a nice living at that), I looked at him a little differently. *He* was one of those guys who made Networkk Marketing *work* for him. Wow! I had tried Primerica years before I met Scott but, as I said, quit too soon because the timing wasn't right. Now here's Scott, who's been at it for over 20 years and has skyrocketing PE. He sets his own hours, inspires others, helps his clients reach their financial goals, and has built a residual income.

Primerica recently spun off from its banking roots to have its own IPO, and Scott benefitted from that as well. I never looked at him with disdain (although others may have). In fact, just the opposite; he commanded my respect. He'd endured all the nonsense 20 years before, with friends and family telling him to quit Network Marketing and get a "real" job. But Scott never wavered, and now he's enjoying the fruits of his labor.

If you don't have high PE, read this book carefully and begin to build it. The more you incorporate the character traits, principles, and techniques of high PE individuals, the more successful you'll become at whatever you do. Then, if you work hard, Network Marketing can provide the platform you need to add the financial piece and eventually gain the free time, and the whole package will send you soaring. You won't believe your good fortune. Well… yes, you will. That's the idea.

> *"Turn fear into faith, doubt into belief and limits into dreams. The key to unlocking your hidden greatness lies within. You are what you think."*
> —Glen Crawford

Read on to see how my own journey evolved and exactly why I think a Network Marketing home-based business may also be *your* ticket to freedom.

Focus on giving smiles away and you will always discover that your own smiles will always be in great supply.

—Joyce Meyer

CHAPTER 5

THE MORE YOU GIVE, THE MORE YOU GET

For thousands of years, scholars and preachers have been telling us how the universe works. I'm not sure about the whole shebang, but one of my core postulates in life and business is: "The more you give, the more you get." I know for a fact this works. It works for me, and I've seen it work over and over again for countless others. Whether they know it or not, I guarantee you that all well-adjusted, self-made, happy, and successful people embody this concept.

This postulate has worked for me all my life, and for many years I didn't even realize it was a technique or skill to be learned. I started off by introducing my friends to each other when I was a kid and then continued all through college. "Hey, I have a good friend who lives around the corner from you, and you guys should meet. You'd get along great." I've seen these connections blossom into great friendships, and I let my friends know early on that if I'm not available, they should get together on their own. I never felt left out—not in the least. Being part of it wasn't why I introduced them in the first place. Some people don't believe this behavior breeds success. They may try it once, but they wait for something good to happen within the next hour or the next day. Others think it's illogical because they can't break it down and make sense out of it. They think it's just a silly good karma superstition. However, we can't explain a lot of things that certainly do work for us. I'm not sure exactly how the Internet works, but I do know how to surf the Web for research. Do I really need to know about all the programming and coding behind the scenes? No, it works fine and serves me well. I simply use it as a tool to get me where I want to go and move on.

Now that I've grown up, I find that one of the best things I can do to achieve business success is to connect people without looking for or expecting anything in return. By connecting people, I mean introducing people who may be able to conduct mutually beneficial business with each other.

It doesn't matter whether you believe or disbelieve in the Law of Attraction; it is always working, either for you or against you.
—Anthony Robbins

In 15+ years, I've introduced countless people over lunch or coffee—an attorney client and friend to a local banker or accountant; a printer or the owner of a copy machine company to a local business owner. If I can, I match them up by personality and/or locale as well as business needs. I simply call it a networking lunch or meeting. I often try to pick up the check too, if they let me.

These personal matchups are far superior to any local networking meeting at a diner, where everyone is just looking for leads and handing out cards. The membership of many of these groups tends to change every few months and often consists of entry-level salespeople. Although these networking groups can help you expand your circle, I suggest you find one with high-level people, preferably business owners only. Attend regularly, and schedule one-on-one off-site meetings as much as possible to get to know people at a deeper level. As you can see, I prefer more personal, high-level networking. Real connections with players who have high PE.

David and His Genuine PE

One of my good friends and mentors from New Jersey is a professional insurance and estate planner named David Konikow. According to my definition of success stated in the Introduction, David is one of the most successful people I've ever met. He understands at a core level the power of connecting people simply for connection's sake. In fact, he has built his entire career on putting people together to chat. The result? David's PE is off the charts. If you mention the name David Konikow in New Jersey, it seems someone always knows him, has heard about him, or better yet, wants to meet him. That's serious personal equity.

David is an equity partner in his insurance firm, and he comes and goes as he pleases. He drives his kids to school, and he coaches baseball and other sports. A top producer in his business, David has earned the right to enjoy his free time and significant income as he and his family see fit.

Was he born to be a success, or did he just find the right path for himself early on? Well, for starters, David is always upbeat and complimentary. In fact, so much so that people like me (born and raised in New York) think at first he's putting on a show—that his overly warm and friendly personality can't possibly be genuine. Sometimes our network of friends jokingly refers to him as "Mr. Rogers." But David is for real. He always takes the time to ask about your family, your health, the kids—and he waits for a real answer. He doesn't want fluff; he really wants to know. I'm not certain you can teach genuine interest in others, but I think it can be gained with the intention to do so.

Developing a *true* interest in people will benefit us because they know if we're faking it. We may have an apparent lack of interest resulting from our need to hurry up and get something done. Slowing down and spending a few minutes getting to know the person behind the business can benefit all of us. Many entry level sales seminars and tapes teach us to write down the names and hobbies of our prospects—but consider the motive.

"How's your daughter enjoying Penn State?" you might ask. But do you ask because you really care, or are you merely showing off that you took notes during your first meeting with this person? I think you'll find that when you rise above superficial pleasantries and develop a genuine interest in what's happening in the other person's life, you'll make a more solid and lasting business connection—and often a friend.

Not that we have to be perfect. Even David has his faults. He tends to overbook himself, and his meetings often run overtime, but that's usually because attendees don't want his meetings to end. He's so engaging that people feel good around him. David lives a charmed life, and in that respect, we want to be like him—a person with genuine PE.

BONANZA DOWN THE LINE

When I set up networking connections, I have nothing to gain in the short term, but I know these influential people now view me in a different way. They see Joe O. as someone who goes out of his way to connect good people for good business, and I am now "long in the favor bank." These business people are scratching their heads, asking themselves two questions. "Why don't I do what Joe does more often? and "Who can I introduce to Joe to help him grow his business?" I may not get a call back with a good introduction for weeks, months, years, or ever—but that's okay. I know I moved in the right direction once again.

Here's just one story about connecting that worked out superbly in the end for me. Back in the late 1990s, I cofounded a company that brought a brand new idea to the Northeast based on an employee leasing concept popular in the south. Called a Professional Employer Organization, or PEO, my company served as an outsourcing solution that enabled small to medium-sized businesses to upgrade their human resources, benefits, and payroll functions. Even though the model was new, it made great sense, and within four years I had a business with annual sales of more than $150 million.

PEOs aggregate thousands of employees and save the business owner significant time and money. In addition, my company provided affordable Fortune 500 benefits and sophistication for smaller businesses that didn't have much buying power and couldn't justify hiring a full-time Human Resources professional.

My role in the partnership was to grow the business (in case you couldn't guess). So I was out there networking all day long and explaining what we did to anyone who would listen. I attended all Chamber of Commerce meetings, political functions, and fundraisers—not just handing out cards, but setting up face-to-face meetings to chat in more depth with the people that were serious about networking.

Along the way, I met a certain banker named Kevin, who seemed to have a networking philosophy similar to mine. He was a senior VP at a major regional bank that had a solid reputation. So we set up a meeting at his bank and just chatted. Our purpose was simply to learn who the perfect referrals were for each other. It was a highly effective match because I needed to meet small business owners with fewer than 100 employees, and he knew a bunch. Kevin offered an excellent product and focused on law firms. My PEO had made significant inroads within the legal community because of the compliance factor we added to the workplace.

I set up many meetings for Kevin. Sometimes I attended the meetings and sometimes I didn't, but he got the business almost every time. Kevin's bank had a superior trust account program, and his banking branches began popping up all over New Jersey. Open late and seven days a week, his fast-growing, customer-friendly banks were revolutionary at the time. I felt I was doing these law firms a real favor by introducing a bank with a product that was easy to use and paid a higher interest rate than others. Due to Kevin's professional skills and my personalized referral, he had an exceptionally high close ratio.

Naturally, Kevin felt obligated to pay back the favor. Every time he met with business owner clients or prospects, he would ask them about their human resources needs and give them my card, trying to obtain appointments for me. I did get some meetings, but because PEO services were a new and radical concept in the late 1990s and the sales cycle often extended from 12 to 18 months, it wasn't a great success story. Had we kept score, Kevin closed about 15 law firms I referred to him, totaling over 100 million dollars in trust accounts. Super for Kevin and his career and certainly my pleasure. Me? I think I closed one small deal and had a few mildly interested leads to get back in touch with the next year. So was I upset? Did I feel cheated? Absolutely not. Kevin had become a friend, and I was happy to see his career grow for him and his family. I had faith in the system. I knew how the rules worked, and was confident my time would come.

A few years later, I decided to sell my interest in the PEO (which, by the way, is still going strong and still gets referrals from me). I took the money and spent some of it to build my dream house for my wife and three children.

So what next? The real estate market was heating up in 2002 and 2003, and I noticed that some of our title agency clients were doing quite well. I was intrigued by the title business for a couple of reasons: 1) the owners of these title agencies were making big money and I was not impressed with their skills, and 2) title insurance in New Jersey is highly regulated and all agencies must charge the exact same fees for a closing. This meant that as long as an agency provided good service, the numbers were all about relationships. So I said to myself, "All about relationships? Game on!"

Title insurance orders in New Jersey come mostly from law firms and lenders. I was already well connected in the legal community, and I had gotten to know a few bankers along the way too. So who was one of the first people I called to get started? My friend Kevin, SVP of one of the most successful banks in the region. You can guess what he said. "You're starting a title agency? Now I can really help you—and in a big way!"

Besides touring me around to all the law firms in his client base, Kevin explained to the executive team how much business I'd referred to the bank over the previous five years. He insisted they put my brand new start-up agency on the preferred title list for his entire banking system.

This single relationship helped my title agency become profitable and efficient right from the start. Not only did we receive a steady stream of business from Kevin's bank, but we gained a lot of credibility when we mentioned we were one of the few title agents approved by that bank.

Back in 1998 to 2001 when I was referring Kevin as much business as I could, I had no idea I was going to make a career change in 2002 to the title world. I also never anticipated that one easy and enjoyable relationship with a certain banker would be so fruitful.

It's true: the more you give, the more you get. Connect people as often and genuinely as you can and you'll build PE that will benefit you somewhere down the line.

Your assignment for today? Make a list of the top 20 most influential and impressive business people you know: the owner of the local fancy restaurant, a lawyer, an accountant, the neighbor across the street who sells life insurance, a financial planner... Ask them to meet you for a cup of coffee to learn more about what they do. If you already have a good lead for them, take action. Send an email to your CPA friend saying you'd like to introduce her to the attorney across the street. The goal? To see how all of you can help each other and increase everyone's PE. Arrange to meet at a local coffee shop for 30 minutes and offer to pay. Run with this concept and watch your PE rise.

Always recognize that human individuals are ends,
and do not use them as means to your end.
—Immanuel Kant

CHAPTER 6

Evolving From Traditional Entrepreneurship to Network Marketing

A s you can see from my experiences mentioned in the previous chapter, I was a traditional business person for many years after my trading career. I was proud to be a classic entrepreneur, taking big risks such as borrowing against my home and/or from a local bank, going without income for as long as it took, signing a lease, and hiring staff. I even found it satisfying to commiserate with other entrepreneurs. I knew having my own business was risky, but I was determined to make it work somehow, some way. I was willing to work 12- to 14-hour days six to seven days a week and fit square pegs into round holes to get my company into the black.

BUILDING FROM THE GROUND UP

In 1997, when I co-founded my PEO, Compensation Solutions, Inc., with my then-partner, Tom Cioffe, we worked incredibly long and hard. We had to do everything on a low budget those first few years. We had a very Spartan attitude and somehow believed that the harder we worked and the more we sacrificed, the sweeter our rewards would be some day—hopefully in the near future.

At the time, my son Alex was two years old and my daughter Stephanie was on the way. One reason I left the rat race of Wall Street was to be closer to home and spend more quality time with my family—but it didn't work out quite that way with my new traditional business.

For the first two years, I rarely had any quality time at home. My wife Annmarie was at home and basically on her own raising the kids. Of course I would spend as much time as possible with them; they'd often sleep in our bed at night and I read them stories, but I always seemed to be behind in my work and looking to get back to the office. This was before the Internet changed all the rules. Working remotely was still a new concept so I had to drive 40 minutes to the office to work on proposals and marketing materials. That was then; more on this in a later chapter.

If Annmarie had not been fully supportive and on board for the venture at hand, I wouldn't have had the freedom of time and money I have today. I give my wife a lot of credit. She always trusted my judgment. Many spouses are not supportive with the family mission and don't have the stomach to spend the family savings to pay for basic needs. I've seen many budding entrepreneurs quit because their husband or wife didn't believe in them 100 percent. Sad but true. Annmarie had great faith in my abilities and vision. Thanks, honey!

But our reality was stark for a while. We had no money coming in, and our two babies still needed food, clothing, diapers, and toys. We still had to pay for family parties and holiday gifts. Vacations? We put those on hold. Annmarie could've gone back to work, but paying for full-time childcare wouldn't have made much sense. I had some savings socked away, but they were quickly evaporating.

BYE-BYE LEXUS, HELLO COROLLA

After I left my last employer, I'd taken over the car lease, and the payments for the gorgeous Lexus were killing me. When the lease was up, I couldn't risk purchasing the car because I knew I might need that money soon to pay the mortgage. I had to give it up and find a much cheaper car to lease. I needed something reliable to drive so I answered one of the "come-on" ads from a local car dealer. The ad read: "Brand New Toyota Corolla, Auto, AC – $99/month." I didn't mind signing a two-year lease and driving a Corolla for a while, especially at that price. Heck, it was almost free compared to my Lexus lease. Besides, it would add to my Spartan story of sacrificing for the future.

Because the price was much lower than all the other dealers, I made sure to call when the dealership opened that Saturday morning to confirm the details. Did the car indeed have automatic transmission with air conditioning? He assured me it did and said they had plenty of them so I should "come on down!" Of course I knew the goal of the ad was just to get people in the door—but Annmarie and I went anyway.

When we arrived with ad in hand, they told us this deal was for manual transmission only (Annmarie doesn't drive a stick shift) and that "auto" meant automatic steering. To get an automatic transmission would add $800 to the sticker price and of course increase the payments. Pure nonsense. But I stuck to my guns and demanded to get what they'd assured me on the phone and at the $99 a month payment.

For over an hour, the managers and salespeople discussed this among themselves. Finally, they asked me if I would sign the lease that day if they delivered what they'd promised over the phone—and I agreed. So they drove around a Corolla the color of lime-green Gatorade. At that point,

Annmarie had gone home and I didn't care. I needed a clean, reliable car and the price was right.

Annmarie and I still laugh whenever we think about that tiny green car—or see a color like it on the road (which is very rare).

Stress Came with Success

We did build Compensation Solutions into a huge success. However, when I recall the sacrifice, heartache, and stress I put myself and my family through to make the business work and create a decent income, I think I must have been nuts. What really got me out of bed every day was not the pride of starting my own business or being a "self-made" man. I didn't buy into all that. I just wanted to make my fortune early so I could have choices in life. In addition, I was attracted to the residual income of a PEO. As I described previously, a PEO is basically a one-stop solution for small to medium-sized businesses, processing payroll, administering benefits, and providing Human Resources expertise. So once we'd built a client base, every week or two when a business ran its payroll, we would get paid.

The challenge back in the late 1990s in the Northeast was that few people had heard of the PEO concept. It had evolved as a natural progression out of employee leasing, which started in Texas and Florida years before that. So I had to jump through hoops to make business owners comfortable with the concept, letting them know it was legal and they wouldn't incur any risk working with us. Most important, the concept would be good for them and their employees because they would have all the benefits and services of a Fortune 500 company, while saving time and money.

So working harder than we wanted to, we built Compensation Solutions, Inc. into a profitable business with a solid reputation. In fact, the company won numerous awards, such as "Best Company to Work for in New Jersey" and was a finalist in the Ernst & Young Entrepreneur of the Year Awards a few years in a row.

However, my day-to-day responsibilities were becoming too burdensome. We had over 50 employees, and I wasn't in love with the business anymore. Although I was making really good money, I was "paper rich," meaning all my net worth was tied up in a privately held business. Our third child, Frankie, was born in 2001, and our house began to feel too small. I was advised that if we were going to move, we should do it while the kids were still young to make it easier on them. So in 2003, I sold my interest back to my partner and some other private investors and used the money to build a nice five-bedroom home in a neighborhood with excellent schools. So it worked out rather well, in a way, but it sure was a long hard ride. I recall years earlier not wanting to attend night school to get my MBA. Little did I know I would end up working almost twice as hard and risk all my savings to earn my real-life "school of hard knocks" entrepreneurial MBA. It sure took a lot of time, effort, and risk. Now I know better. It doesn't have to be that way. Man, I wish I'd known more about home-based businesses back then.

A NEW AND PROSPEROUS VENTURE... UNTIL...

Compensation Solutions happened to process payroll for a few title insurance agencies, and I noticed these agencies were doing extremely well. In the last chapter, I mentioned that because of New Jersey regulations, success in the title industry was all about service and relationships—so I decided to get involved (relationships being my strong suit). If I could bring in the business and hire a few top-notch administrators, I knew we'd lead the pack.

At this point, I approached my good friends Bart Oates, Esq. and Frank Marone. As you may know, Bart is an attorney and three-time Super Bowl Champion. I'd already made him a minority owner and board member of Compensation Solutions, but he wasn't very active in any day-to-day advisory services. Because I'd be courting other attorneys to use our title services, Bart would be a great partner for the new venture. I'd known Frank Marone since the late 1980s from my Wall Street trading days. At the time, he'd been asked to take another pay cut so he was looking to make a career change. Frank and I always got along famously, and I was very comfortable with his business ethics, having been in the trenches with him for so many years. I knew that all three of us lived by that ethical business code: "My word is my bond—period."

They both agree to come on board, so we started dropping in on attorneys and lenders throughout northern New Jersey, and people were happy to give us a shot. After a few years went by, one day I got several voicemails congratulating me on All-Pro Title being named one of the top 10 title insurance agencies in the state in a New Jersey business magazine. The publication had interviewed me a while back, and I had honestly forgotten all about it.

So we were rocking and rolling—but I'd gotten lured away from one of my own rules; I was no longer in a residual business. Every month was a new month, and we had to start from scratch. Payroll processing had been residual; title transactions were not. It didn't matter much for about five years, as we rode the housing boom until late 2008. Then business almost came to a standstill. We were paying our bills at home but not getting ahead. So there I was—a guy with a colossal Personal Equity rating—once again a victim of circumstance. This time it wasn't due to technology or bank mergers—it was the economy. How did I let this happen to me? I vowed to never let it happen again. I was back seeking a new opportunity.

MY RETURN TO NETWORK MARKETING

In the summer of 2008, one of my loan officer buddies, Mike Moore, kept hounding Frank and me to meet with him to see a business plan. He was well trained because he wouldn't tell me much about it up front. He said we needed to get together in person. After putting it off for a while, we finally set a meeting for 1:00 p.m. on a Wednesday. I was coming from another appointment and was hungry so I checked to see if Frank would be there to greet Mike. I didn't want to feel bad about showing up late (isn't that what partners are for?).

As it turned out, I missed the meeting completely, but Frank signed both of us up anyway. It was only $448, and Mike was a good client so I didn't think much of it. The business was a cash-back Web portal business with thousands of major stores that paid residuals on members' ongoing shopping and the purchases of others we got to sign up for their own shopping portal. It was Network Marketing. Something I'd avoided for the previous 20 years since for my brief foray into Primerica. However, this opportunity was a little different because the company had no proprietary product. The deal involved shopping online and getting cash back. We were required to spend $100 a month on natural, healthy, and "green" products, but we could choose from thousands of brand name items you'd find at most supermarkets. They were a little more expensive through the program, but this was necessary to get commissions so it wasn't a major objection. Besides, I shopped almost exclusively online anyway. When my kids were little, I dreaded going to the mall and dealing with car seats and strollers so I'd cruise the Web and buy stuff after they went to bed. Frank and I already spent a lot of money buying office supplies and paper for the title agency. The cash back on just one on-line store alone would more than pay for the sign-up fees.

Long story short, Frank and I quickly became top producers in that business. We invited our attorney and loan officer friends to see the model and it exploded. As the top money earners in the Northeast, we made over $500,000 in under 18 months. Lots of people were impressed—astounded, in fact—by our success, but it didn't faze us. We treated it like any other business and got paid accordingly. In addition, we realized that this "new" model of home-based business had some great legs. No overhead, no risk… it was the future. We learned a great deal about ourselves and how to motivate people and to always keep our eyes and ears open for a high-potential opportunity. Plus, we understood that traditional business owners like us could be the future budding superstars in home-based businesses—if they could just "see" it.

However, premium cash-back shopping Web portals became an increasingly tougher sale. Big banks and Web search engines began to offer "free" portals that made us feel uneasy about our long-term growth.

EUREKA!

As this new sea change was threatening to swamp us, we sought to meet with a good buddy of ours to share our respective business models. He had left the mortgage business while it was still rocking to sell energy in New York (even though he lived in New Jersey). His was a Network Marketing model as well, so we wanted to show him our new business to get his opinion, and of course we hoped he would like what he saw. However, we also wanted to learn why he was so enamored with his energy business.

Well, when Frank and I met with him, he told us he didn't shop online, so our business wasn't for him—but *everyone* uses electricity and gas. How could we argue? Frank and I immediately signed up with him, even though the model had not yet come to our home state. We all distinctly recall me saying to Frank, "If the energy business comes to New Jersey, we'll retire in two years."

As we waited and waited for the company to come to our state, we soon got word of another company in Connecticut that had more immediate plans to launch in New Jersey. In addition, it was *green* energy. Frank and I had learned to become more environmentally conscious from our green online shopping business, so this also resonated well with us—in fact, better than any of the other energy companies out there. People will do only so much to make a buck, but if it's for a good cause, they'll be motivated to follow through on a consistent basis.

We joined on with Viridian Energy before it was even licensed in New Jersey. In addition, our buddy loved the model and the management team so much that even *he* joined up. We were blown away by the potential of green energy, deregulation, and a completely untapped market converging right here in our backyard. The statistics were mind boggling. Viridian had plans to spread into multiple states with similar attractive demographics. It was almost effortless for people to become customers. I had a chance to participate in the $500 billion energy deregulation movement… all while reducing our carbon footprint. Now *here* was an opportunity!

Frank and I jumped in 100 percent and quickly became the company's biggest producers. We're now regarded as being among the few top network marketing experts in the world. Besides the monthly residual income, I've grown to love the low overhead and unlimited profits of the Network Marketing model. Before I'd taken another serious look at this business model, I didn't realize you could truly make millions of dollars a year while helping others. I've seen a new trend developing. "Traditional" business owners with employees, long leases, insurance, and other such limitations are now flocking to quality Network Marketing businesses such as The Viridian Network.

My advice to these traditional entrepreneurs is simple: If you're the type of person who always finds yourself in the top five to ten percent of your field, *then get involved with a quality network marketing company* for the reasons I've explained. I don't know about you, but I'm very tired of the aggravation of running a typical business. I've said many times that even if you handed me a successful franchise for free, I would politely decline. You could offer me a business worth $1 million with a proven track record on a busy corner, and I would rather stick with my Network Marketing business. When you have high Personal Equity, you get to choose. Let this be your motivation to get busy and build the power of your PE.

*Immaturity is the incapacity to use one's intelligence
without the guidance of another.*
—Immanuel Kant

CHAPTER 7

WHY A HOME-BASED BUSINESS?

C an real people make real money with these "too good to be true" businesses? For over 20 years, I didn't believe it—even though I knew a few people who made it work for them. I always had a deep respect for these people because I knew it wasn't easy. Nothing worthwhile in life is easy, right? But making more money than ever before from the comfort of your own home? Lounging around in your workout clothes while others commute back and forth to work? Is it being done? Can it be done? I wondered…

So for a long time, I completely disregarded these types of businesses. Not that I didn't think they were legit. I knew Amway and Primerica were legendary mega-businesses, so unlike many others, I never had any close-minded ideas that they were all "pyramid schemes."

A Similar Model

Actually, the typical home-based business model of leveraging the work of others and pay based on self-starter productivity mimics the model used by your local real estate brokers and agents. Did you buy your home from an undercover agent for a pyramid scheme? After all, the real estate broker holds the license and gets a cut from any and all property sold by his network of multi-level freelance agents. Some agents list the home and bring the buyer and get paid most of the 5–6 percent commission, but the broker always gets his share for setting up the operation. A real estate agent who hustles and makes a lot of connections can make more than a decent living buying and selling houses for clients. At the end of the year, they can surely make more than their broker. In addition, there's nothing stopping them from spinning off and becoming a broker themselves. Some successful agents aspire to become a broker someday, and others enjoy just being an agent. They like their side of the system because they have fewer worries, minimal overhead, and a pure pay-for-performance business model.

However, as you know, this model of real estate brokerage in which the broker leverages the time and efforts of his or her agents isn't completely home-based. Often the broker has a local office that the agents use as their base—but they don't make their money sitting in the office pushing paper. It's about networking, making connections. The higher the agent's PE, the more sales he or she can make.

The Benefits

So why a home-based business? Well, first of all, the United States today has two tax systems—one for the business owners with all the write-offs and one for the working stiffs. I'm fortunate to live in an affluent neighborhood in northern New Jersey where it isn't uncommon for people to make $200,000, $500,000, or even $1 million a year. Some of these people are corporate executives and some are business owners. The difference? The corporate exec making $500K a year in W-2 paychecks takes home only about 65 percent of it, or $325,000. That means a tax payment of $175,000 a year! The tax system greatly favors the business owner, who with liberal write-offs, may be able to take home 75–85 percent. That's a significant difference. I'm not giving tax advice here, but it's not unusual for business owners to write off all or at least part of their cars, phones, and travel and other related expenses.

Another reason for a home-based pay-for-performance business is you learn a lot about yourself—your talents and weaknesses. The Network Marketing model demands personal development. So as you build your own business, you add equity by both the standard definition and my PE definition every day. How will this help you? People with high PE will always thrive at whatever they attempt to do, and they end up in the top five to ten percent of the crowd. The cream of the crop. If you already have high PE and you aim to become an overachiever, a "top-percenter," an "outlier," then you may want to seriously consider a quality Network Marketing company. Or perhaps you want to keep developing your PE further to gain more control over your success and a higher standard of living. There again, a quality Network Marketing company is your best bet because the lifestyle and satisfaction are unmatched. I know this to be true for me in my Viridian Energy business.

That said, the single best reason to own a home-based business is the freedom it provides. You can *work less and make more every year.* Although this goal is quite difficult to achieve in traditional brick-and-mortar businesses, it has been done. If you can set up your shop with talented people you trust, you can work part-time and make the lion's share of the money. Frank and I basically did that for a long while with All-Pro Title during the good years. We hired excellent staff, we paid them well, including cars and benefits, and we took prospects out for lunch and brought in the business. I'm proud to say that although I have my title insurance license and can talk about title at some length, I could never have gotten behind a desk and processed any title commitments. I didn't even know how to log in to our title software program!

Well-paid and admired corporate executives—whether they're with a Fortune 500 manufacturing or technology company, law firm, or big bank—can never work less and make more. At least not for long. In the corporate business world, you're likely to hear: "We're paying you $500K a year. We need to see you working at least 50 hours a week." You can become an expert in your field and create systems and efficiencies, and they only want more. Let's say you take a flailing department and completely turn it around. It was barely breaking even, and now, thanks to you, it's a profit center making $5 million a year. You may get a one-time bonus and a nice thank you, but now they want you to go do it again for another department—or worse: "Thanks and there's the door! We don't need you anymore… mission accomplished."

With your own business, if you get the profitability up to a certain amount, you reap all the rewards and you *cannot* be fired. In fact, once you build up a residual home-based business, you may not have much to do—except perhaps teach what you know as a way of giving back.

NOW IS THE TIME

Perhaps I never fully understood home-based businesses because I was always approached by entry-level newbies who didn't do a good job of convincing me they were viable options. The few meetings I attended were with reputable companies that have tripled in size since the 1990s. One of those businesses was Primerica Financial Services. As you may recall, I attended a few local meetings and even studied for and received my insurance

> *"The tipping point is that magic moment when an idea, trend, or social behavior crosses a threshold, tips, and spreads like wildfire."*
> —Malcolm Gladwell

license. However, I quit after a few months because (I know now) I was lacking the conviction needed to succeed in a big way. I wasn't "all-in." Although I knew the guy drawing circles in front of the room was being honest about his residual income and the "sky's the limit opportunity," I just wasn't ready—mentally, physically, or spiritually.

I do regret not being more focused and open-minded at the time. I may have been retired by now if I'd gotten serious about Network Marketing 15 years ago. But without the Internet, email, and cell phones, it would've taken a lot of time and effort to work a second business from home and keep it alive and prosperous—even if I *had* been ready.

Today, with all the communication tools available, a home-based business makes all the sense in the world. Years ago, we had to rely on a big company to house the servers, and long-distance calls were expensive, while today these costs are negligible. Why commute every day when you can get 80 percent of your work done at home around your own schedule?

The tide is turning fast within corporate America. People are tired of seeing CEOs who make $150 million a year run companies that are losing money. Why is one person making that much anyway? How could he or she possibly be worth that kind of pay? I'm all for corporate profits and the free enterprise system; however, I'd rather see a company pay 300 independent people working from home $500K a year than pay an exorbitant amount to one hotshot flying around in a corporate jet. Plus, these hotshots know full well that if they do a lousy job and get fired, they'll get an enormous severance package. Spreading the wealth not only benefits the company because pay is based on performance, but it's better for entrepreneurs, investors, the economy, and of course, family life.

Over the last 200 years, the Western world has gone from the farming era to the Industrial Age to the Information Age. With the launching of the railroads and mass production, we saw huge wealth creation during the 50-year period after the Civil War. We recognize the names: Rockefeller, Mellon, Vanderbilt, Ford, Edison, and so on. A few select leaders established dynasties by creating millions of jobs, mostly for factory workers. In fact, entire cities and towns exist today only because a business tycoon decided to set up shop there (e.g., Detroit, Michigan, Pittsburgh, Pennsylvania…). These movers and shakers dictated salaries, owned the banks that lent money for local housing, and also built that housing. For many, a factory job was a dream come true. No more long hours in the fields with no money in their pockets. Now they could live in a city or town and work and chat side by side with people creating useful and cutting-edge widgets. This signaled major progress, especially for the masses.

Then came the Information Age around World War II, when the phone, radio, and TV started becoming mainstream and people became much more informed. The 1960 presidential campaign began the practice of a televised formal debate—the first time millions of people got to see their candidates live and in action. Many historians claim that JFK won the election because he looked more clean-cut and trustworthy than Nixon with his five o'clock shadow. A few decades later, the Information Age took off in the late 1990s with the World Wide Web. Today, we rely on search engines and have endless sources for research at our fingertips.

We surely live in a world of great abundance. To make money, you need to create value. Unique value. So how can you do that? Do you want to compete with the geniuses who are increasing the power of the microchip? Would you advise a straight-A student to go into computer science today and hopefully years from now come up with a better program or motherboard? Not me! I wouldn't want anyone I know personally to take on the brilliant, hard-working, and inexpensive laborers in the Asian markets. If you're a number-cruncher or computer programmer, you'll *always* find someone or *something* that can do what you do better, faster, or cheaper. I say uncle. Hats off to them! Let them have their victory and let me use their tools.

The phrase to "think outside the box" has become a cliché, but it's never been more important. Innovation and open-mindedness are crucial for both the evolution of society and personal growth. To advance the world, we need both those who create our technology and those who use it creatively.

If your goals are to have more money, freedom, and satisfaction in life, build your PE. Then, with today's technologies, you can work from home if you choose, and achieve whatever you aspire to. Some people make a few extra hundred dollars a month this way to help supplement their income, and others make many times more than they ever could with a traditional job.

Whether you go into Internet marketing, consulting, other online or over-the-phone services, or network marketing, you'll no longer need a formal office space, a commute, and a regular "nine-to-five" regimen. When you develop your Personal Equity, *you* get to decide how and where you want to create your wealth.

I don't care how much power, brilliance or energy you have, if you don't harness it and focus it on a specific target, and hold it there you're never going to accomplish as much as your ability warrants.

—*Zig Ziglar*

CHAPTER 8

SEE IT AND YOU'LL BE IT

You may well have found your niche, and perhaps you'd rather not start a home-based business. However, please know that *whatever* you want to do in life will be enhanced by building your PE and using the principles presented in this book. In Chapter 1, my personal story illustrated the universal law that what you want badly enough and focus on, you'll manifest in your life. Long before I learned about this Law of Attraction from others, I knew the principle to be true, to be self-evident. I knew that if I imagined something—visualized it

THE POWER OF PERSONAL EQUITY

happening in my mind's eye, with enough emotional intensity, I could make it happen.

Even as a little kid, I always felt as if I had the power to control my future—just like I sometimes had the power to design my dreams at night. Have you ever experienced this? I recall that at a young age I'd occasionally notice something odd in the middle of a dream—like seeing someone who'd been dead for a while or being in the house I grew up in but hadn't seen in years. That's when I'd realize that what I was experiencing wasn't real, that it must be a dream. So I decided to have some fun with this—to design a plot. I'd "fly" across the country, feeling the wind blow through my hair as I looked down at the landscape. It felt so amazingly real. I'd keep telling myself to remain calm because if I got too excited I'd wake up. This would often last only a few seconds—if I was lucky maybe a full minute—but it was a great feeling.

Has this ever happened to you? I looked up this phenomenon, and it's called lucid dreaming. People have created techniques on how to prolong a dream and get better at designing your nightly adventures. To me, lucid dreaming is great proof of how powerful our mind is and how we can indeed manipulate our reality.

If we can manipulate our dreams, why can't we also affect our daydreams—our goals—and make them become real? Why can't we focus on what we'd like to see happen and make it so? Perhaps the process isn't an exact science, but it may be. I do know it works to some degree, and to me, it's not a stretch. I can't tell you how many times I intentionally create events and then celebrate the outcomes. Sometimes I look back to see if I can determine what I was thinking to manifest an event—good or bad.

Can you think of an event that took place in your life, good or bad, and determine that you focused on it, intentionally or unintentionally, and actually made it happen?

MANIFESTING A REAL-LIFE DREAM

I'll share with you something that happened in my life that I feel I affected long ago. It had to do with a part-time Major League

Baseball player named Benny Ayala, and it began in 1974 when I was eight years old.

I started to fall in love with baseball back in 1973, when I was only seven. My dad grew up in Brooklyn and was a big Brooklyn Dodgers fan. He naturally became a New York Mets fan after the Dodgers left for Los Angeles, considering the hated Yankees were *not* an option. Mets fans are a tough and loyal group. We've endured a lot of heartache over the years, sprinkled with a few great successes that seemed to come only once every generation. It's not easy living in the same town as the most successful team in all of sports if you're a fan of the other team.

Even casual sports fans know the story of the 1969 Miracle Mets. These lovable losers, who began in 1962 as an expansion team and never had a winning season for seven years, shocked the universe and became world champions. They beat the heavily favored Baltimore Orioles four games to one. This happened in October of 1969, just a few months after we put a man on the moon. Coincidence? I don't think so! It was a highly inspirational time. People were feeling that anything was possible.

I was only three years old when this occurred, but when the Mets made it back in 1973, I was ready. At the age of seven, I was all in—sleeping with my Mets batting glove, which I got at my first game in Shea Stadium.

I vividly recall sitting in Sister Lawrence's third grade class at St. Theresa's school on Staten Island. She had handed out Rosary beads and was teaching us how to pray the Holy Rosary. This was the fall of 1973. The Mets were trying to make it to the World Series again, and these Rosary beads would definitely get them there.

It worked! The Mets beat the mighty Cincinnati Reds, aka the "Big Red Machine," and then had to face the mighty Oakland A's. The A's were already world champions, and once again, the Mets were lucky to be there. So it worked! I prayed the Rosary and the Mets made it to the World Series. But here's the problem: I was only seven, and I was just beginning to figure out this whole manifestation thing. I should've been more *specific* and prayed that they *win* the World Series. But it was too late—so guess what happened... they lost.

Now, of course today I don't think I possess some kind of crazy power over the universe—or that whatever people specifically ask for will simply happen. Heck, I'm sure lots of kids in Cincinnati were also praying and hoping their beloved Reds would beat the Mets and make it to the World Series. However, I do believe that at age seven this was a healthy belief to have. In fact, it's a healthy belief for us at any age, as long as our dreams and wishes don't hurt anyone else. Why would it be okay for a young kid to dream but not okay for adults? We need to get back to those big dreams and the "anything is possible" attitude. We adults are way too pragmatic. Fact is, there's indeed a little magic that we can't explain in visualization techniques. My advice? Simply accept that they work and let them serve you.

Even though the Mets lost that Series, I was hooked on baseball for good. I couldn't wait until next year. Those of you who follow baseball know that "wait 'til next year" is a common phrase in the sport. "Next year" everyone gets a fresh start and all possibilities are renewed. If you happen to be a Mets fan, you can certainly relate.

BENNY AYALA

Then came 1974, and at the age of eight, I set a goal to watch every inning of every Mets game. Of course I didn't even come close because I was just a kid; I had homework and wasn't in charge of the TV (like I am now, for the most part). But I did watch a lot of the games. One particular game that really had an impact on me happened on August 27, 1974. The Mets weren't doing well and a lot of fans had stopped watching the games. Because the team was already way behind in the standings, the season wasn't going to end up with a playoff run. In fact, the Mets didn't see the playoffs again for another 10+ years.

I recall reading in the morning newspaper that day about a rookie who showed some promise. The Mets had called him up to the big leagues to start that night's game in left field. The article in the paper did a great job of reminding people how difficult it was to make it to the major leagues. Even at the age of eight, I understood the magnitude of this first game for a young player named Benny Ayala. How cool it must be to finally make it to the big leagues! Would he be nervous? Would he strike out? Would he be a superstar who could change the Mets' season? Or would he fizzle out like so many other players? I made it a point to watch the game that night.

When Benny got up, the announcers mentioned that this was indeed his first at bat in the majors. I was nervous for him. I was wondering if I would be nervous when I made it to the major leagues for my first at bat. (Remember when you were young? All things were possible.)

So what happened when Mr. Benigno Ayala got to bat for the first time? He hit a home run! He floated around the bases with a huge smile. I recall being so happy for him. (I'm getting chills as I think about it.) Not only had he joined an elite group of people who can say they played in the major leagues, but he'd also joined a far more exclusive group of players who hit a home run their first time at bat. Major League Baseball has been around for well over 100 years, and in 1974, that elite group numbered fewer than 70.

I recall screaming and yelling and running upstairs to tell my mom and dad. I couldn't wait to share the story with my friends at school the next day. That night and so many days and nights afterwards, I daydreamed of hitting a home run my first major league at bat—someday soon. Yes, I was not only going to play Major League Baseball someday for the New York Mets at Shea Stadium, but I was also going to hit a home run my first chance. Why not? I'm eight years old.

Decades later, whenever I stumble upon a fellow rabid Mets fan at a barbecue or business meeting, I always bring up my trivia question: Who was the first Met to hit a home run in his first major league at bat? Some do get it right.

THE STORY HITS HOME(R)

So why did I bring up this story about Benny Ayala who went on to play another ten years part-time and hit only 38 career home runs? Was it just to inspire you and remind you to keep dreaming? Of course not. There's more to this story.

As you can probably guess, I never made it to the major leagues. I was, however, a very good player. At the age of 15, I was selected for a New York City all-star team and played in Japan and Taiwan all summer. After high school, I accepted a scholarship to play Division I baseball at Rutgers University.

The dream died after one year when my elbow began bothering me to the point that I was a candidate for "Tommy John" surgery, a type of elbow ligament reconstruction. However, back in 1984 this procedure was still experimental and certainly not available to college kids. In addition to the nagging pain, serious baseball was becoming a little boring for me and involved lots of bus rides and double headers during final exam week in May. Although I saw good playing time for a freshman, I didn't like the rigid schedule so I decided to give up my scholarship and focus on my grades. I loved the freedom to work out on my own schedule—which led to my amateur bodybuilding pursuits during college. I was attracted to bodybuilding because it was very competitive and goal-oriented. I knew it would teach me a lot about self-discipline.

So my dream of making it to the big leagues died, and the specific dream of hitting a home run my first at bat at Shea Stadium died too… or did it? Fast forward exactly 30 years to the summer of 2004. I was president of All-Pro Title Agency in Morristown, New Jersey, and I got a call from one of my clients at JP Morgan Chase. The bank was having a client appreciation day at Shea Stadium, and due to my high PE, I was offered two tickets. Technically, Chase was my client and I should have been giving *them* tickets to events. However, a few of the top lending executives at the bank knew I was a rabid Mets fan who'd greatly appreciate the gesture. Turns out the bank had rented Shea Stadium (the Mets were out of town) and invited a group of about 50 bank clients to play a pickup game on the Shea Stadium diamond. How cool was that?! I decided to use the extra ticket to invite a prospective attorney client to build goodwill for my title agency. As I went through my contact list, I searched for a legitimate Mets fan. I didn't want to waste this opportunity to play at my favorite stadium on some unappreciative Yankees fan.

I called the managing partner of a law firm I was courting in Hackensack. He was a Yankee fan. Did he know of any serious Mets fans at his firm who would truly appreciate a day in the sun at Shea? He gave me the name of a young attorney, Angelo Bagnara. I called Angelo and left a voice mail about the details of the event, along with some Mets trivia questions. I let him know his boss was giving him the day off and I'd pick him up Tuesday at 9:30 a.m. to drive to Flushing, New York.

I was 38 years old at the time, and I hadn't picked up a ball or swung a bat in over 15 years. After college I'd played a little baseball in my early 20s, but that seemed like ages ago. I'd stayed in good shape, though, and was a home run hitter back in the day. Was this my chance?

I picked up Angelo that day and we made small talk, chatting baseball all the way into Queens from New Jersey. I also gave him an education in real music as I made him listen to Led Zeppelin and Steely Dan—two bands he couldn't identify. In passing, I said, "If I get a good pitch, I could hit a home run today." He later told me he thought I was completely nuts. *Who the heck does this old man think he is? Shea Stadium is one of the most difficult parks to hit a home run in for major leaguers, and this guy who hasn't played in years thinks he's going to do it today?* In addition, we didn't know how much action we would even get. The whole idea was to network, have a little fun, and not get hurt.

When we arrived at Shea, we were given Mets jerseys and introduced to some of the legends from the 1969 team: Joe Pignatano, Ed Charles, Art Shamsky, Ed Kranepool, and my favorite pitcher of the 1970s, Craig Swan. "Swannie" was the Mets' best pitcher during the lean years after they traded away the legendary Tom Seaver—which by the way happened on my 11th birthday—ugh!

So we split up and started batting practice. When they dumped a bag of old wooden bats, Angelo said hitting a home run would be impossible. Aluminum bats like the ones we used in college allowed a batter to add distance to the ball. Wooden bats, especially "dead" ones that had been lying around for a while, were not going to be helpful. Plus, I got stuck with ancient Joe Pignatano throwing me ten pitches for my batting practice session. He threw the ball so slowly it barely reached the plate. I swung as hard as I could while still trying to keep my form and hit a few long fly balls but nothing even close to the fences. When we broke for lunch, they told us we'd be playing a "real" game after we finished eating.

For the game, they brought in a college kid who could throw consistent strikes to keep the game moving. I was finally up in the third inning. The first pitch came right down the middle—and yes, you guessed it. I hit the ball over the fence and into the visitor's bullpen! Don't believe it? Just check *Joe's HR at Shea!.mov* on YouTube. I was very lucky that JP Morgan Chase actually filmed the day's events, and I eventually got my hands on the video. My brother John added music and posted it (along with a few sarcastic remarks).

The fantasy I'd envisioned over and over again almost exactly 30 years before had in fact come true. It wasn't exactly a major league game, but it was indeed my first game ever at Shea Stadium—and I did hit a home run over the fence. Crazy story, right? Did I hit this home run because I envisioned it so vividly as a kid, or was this just a remarkable coincidence? Heck, playing at Shea Stadium was a dream come true in itself. How many people ever get to play ball on the field of their favorite team? But me? Not only did I get to play, but I fulfilled a lifetime dream to hit a homer in my first at bat—just like Benny Ayala.

Another special thing happened that day. I met my now very close friend Angelo Bagnara, Esq., whom I hired soon afterward to run my title agency—and he still runs the office today.

Thank you, Benny Ayala, for your inspiration!

YOU CAN DO IT TOO

Now of course I can't explain how 30 years after my childhood dream I got a call to play baseball at Shea Stadium (although people with high PE seem to get invited to cool events, so be prepared). And I certainly can't explain actually hitting a home run that day. The odds are literally astronomical. However, I don't need to explain it—and neither do you. I can't explain how my cell phone works, and I'm not even interested in knowing how it works. I just need to know *how to work it*. A cell phone is a proven, invaluable tool that makes our lives easier. I can just accept this and move on.

So why not simply accept these visualization techniques and the laws of attraction and focus as proven tools, then go ahead and use them to serve you? Whatever you focus on will come about in some way, shape, or form.

Be careful, though, because this can work for negative outcomes as well. When I got to bat that day, after bragging at lunch to Angelo and others about what a big star I was as a kid, I could've just as easily focused on just not striking out and looking bad. But if I had focused on not striking out instead of hitting a long home run, it would have greatly increased my chances of striking out. I know a home run would never have happened with that visual running through my head.

What are some of the lofty goals you have for yourself and your career? Write them down and focus on them. Picture your success. Do you want to double your salary while working less? That's a good start. Do you want to have your own private jet plane someday? One thing I can assure you: People who have enough wealth to own their personal jet definitely use these techniques in some form and so can you.

A man should never be appointed into a managerial position if his vision focuses on people's weaknesses rather than on their strengths.

—Peter Drucker

CHAPTER 9

CHOOSE YOUR MENTORS CAREFULLY

While you're visualizing the success you want, choose mentors who can show you the way. What are mentors? Simply put, mentors are people from whom we learn certain knowledge, skills, or character traits. They share with us what they know by giving advice and sometimes through example. We've all heard people giving their mentors credit when they receive awards for achievement: "I owe my success to my dad," or "I wouldn't have achieved this award if it hadn't been for my eighth-grade teacher," or "I'd like to thank my business coach for helping me to excel."

While many people call all-time greats such as Abe Lincoln or Nelson Mandela mentors, these icons serve to inspire rather than mentor. I think of mentors as contemporaries you can interact with on any given day—people you can meet with or at least call and talk with on the phone. They have certain natural traits or skills you'd like to develop, and you can just observe them or chat with them to see what you can learn. They don't even have to know they're part of your mentor portfolio. You can let them know if you like, but they may feel uncomfortable and self-conscious if you ask them to "mentor" you, and it could change the whole dynamic of your relationship. However, you could say something like, "Hey, Francesca; you're always so organized. Would you be willing to let me in on your secrets?"

Mentors can be a source of guidance and inspiration, and they can help you make your way through life with greater ease and success. If you choose them carefully, they will be the people whose character and success in certain areas you wish to emulate. They've learned a thing or two, often from their mentors, but sometimes the hard way through trial and error. A good mentor knows how to pass on knowledge and skill so the next guy (which may be you) doesn't have to reinvent the wheel. Mentors can save you time and error and help you through when you're feeling discouraged.

DIFFERENT MENTORS FOR DIFFERENT REASONS

Sometimes the right mentors happen to be part of your life (your uncle teaches you how to play baseball), or they appear when you need them (your co-worker shows you an easy way to do those reports you've been dreading). Other times you have to seek them out; but don't despair because mentors are everywhere and can appear in many forms. Just don't expect your mentors to be good at everything you need to know. For example, people may come to me for certain kinds of business advice and to learn how to build personal equity, but I sure wouldn't be able to advise them on how to organize files. I'd send them to "Francesca" for that!

I suggest you take the best qualities from the people around you and create the perfect fictional mentor. For instance, one I use combines the visionary skills of a bright, young executive such as Viridian Energy founder and CEO, Michael Fallquist, with the carefree playfulness of my 10-year-old son, Frankie. Using these two as inspiration allows me to focus on what needs to get done now to create a bright future as well as chill out and have fun when something doesn't work the way I want it to during the day. I'm not saying Michael Fallquist doesn't have a playful side. I know he does; but I don't get to see it often during the business day when we interact, and I certainly don't think he can compete with a 10-year-old boy in that category. I shoot for extremes so I can end up where I need to be.

List Your Mentors

Create a foundation for your mentor list by first writing down certain qualities, skills, or activities you want to develop or improve. Perhaps you'd like to be on time for appointments or become better at letting people know you appreciate them. Keep searching for traits that will enhance your personal equity.

Then list people who embody these traits or qualities. Think about what makes them good at these functions and emulate them. Again, they don't have to be people you want to be like in every respect—just in that quality. You may know someone who self-sabotages his career and can't hold down a job but lights up a room every time he enters it. What does he do to create that bright aura?

Don't fake something that doesn't feel right for you, but decide what you want to develop and work at making it your own. Combine the actions and traits of several people that fit you best. Not only will you magnetize people to you, but you'll lift your own spirits—all to the good of your personal equity.

When searching for someone to help you with your daily attitude, keep in mind that anyone might fit your criteria. Perhaps it's the security guard in the building where you work. Man! you often think to yourself; Charlie is always in a good mood! Cheery and friendly, rain or shine. He must have his life challenges, but he doesn't seem to let them bother him.

Learn from Charlie.

MENTORS IN MY LIFE

Besides Michael Fallquist and my son Frankie, I've had countless mentors in my life, and many of them don't realize the extent of their influence. My parents stand front and center among the crowd. With my dad's hard work in law enforcement with the NYPD and FBI, he taught me how to always be consistent and reliable. My mom worked part-time as a legal secretary for a few different law firms. Although some of the attorneys were kind and considerate, others were absolutely abusive. Determined to keep a level head through it all, she earned extra money so her kids could attend private schools and get generous gifts on holidays. When I feel the daily grind getting to me, my parents serve as mentors as I recall their determination, hard work, and uncomplaining sacrifice.

I'm constantly seeking to emulate the best qualities of successful people I know. One of my mentors (who didn't know he was until I interviewed him for this book) is Glen Stevens, CEO of Gain Capital (NYSE: GCAP). Glen was a senior foreign exchange trader and director in the 1980s and '90s and worked at several highly prestigious banks and investment houses. I had the pleasure of having drinks and dinner with him from time to time over the years. I knew he had an Ivy League MBA and was well respected, but I didn't know he had such high PE. During my days on Wall Street, MBAs were everywhere. Some were charismatic visionaries with great street smarts and some were duds. Although they obviously all performed well on their standardized exams and in the classroom, many would put you to sleep with their over-analytical minds and theories. This skill set wasn't ideal for high-pressure, "go-with-your-gut" billion dollar trading. Glen Stevens was one of the few who had all the bases covered. In addition, he was a true entrepreneur at heart, with that special talent to see a trend before it starts and jump on the opportunity.

While most of the established FX traders were happy to be making great salaries and taking four weeks of vacation, Glen wanted more. He wanted to build something for himself—and others—and recognized a great opportunity to take the trillion dollar institutional foreign exchange markets to the little guy. He was part of the movement that introduced Wall Street to Main Street. Stocks and bonds had already made the transition in the 1980s with companies such as Fidelity Investments and Charles Schwab. Glen wanted to create a similar business model for currency trading and started searching for an opportunity. He met up with a few other like-minded visionaries and in 1999 cofounded a company called Gain Capital.

With his high PE, Glen was able to surround himself with other talented and trustworthy people from the New York trading markets, whether they were employees, brokers who worked for him, or rival traders who were worthy adversaries. When you have plenty of Personal Equity, you attract the talent. There are always people who will trust and listen to you.

Glen could have stayed in New York City and played it safe, moving on up the corporate ladder. However, we now know that *safe is the new risky.* Glen saw all the benefits of growing his own business—the potential financial upside and the opportunity to take people along with him. Most importantly from my perspective, he founded this business in the suburbs of New Jersey where he lives. His goal? To create a profitable business *close to his family.*

Can we have it all? Most people don't think it's possible, but Glen knew it was. His dream was to establish a pioneering retail FX business and grow it to such a huge success that it could someday go public. Why not?

Well sure enough, in 2010, after about 10 years of viral growth, opening offices in New York, London, Tokyo, Hong Kong, Sydney, Seoul, and Singapore, and servicing over 140 countries, Gain Capital went public. Clearly, ringing the bell that day at the New York Stock Exchange with his team was a wonderful experience—a dream come true, an ultimate goal fully achieved.

However, Glen will tell you it's the journey along the way that matters most and that overcoming the many challenges during a growth period makes you who you are. Would Glen be the same person today if he'd never ventured out of corporate America to do his own thing? Probably not. If Gain Capital had never taken off the way it did or had failed after a few years, would it have been worth taking the chance—worth all the time and effort? The answer is a resounding YES. Although Glen was talented enough to make this eventually work for him in a big way, I'm sure he wanted the company to go public even sooner than it did, and he no doubt has even loftier goals that are yet to be achieved. Nevertheless, Glen Stevens's Personal Equity keeps climbing.

As you can see, some of my mentors are visionaries, such as Michael Fallquist, CEO of Viridian Energy, and Glen Stevens, CEO of Gain Capital. Both of these bright young men started businesses that were at least a decade ahead of their time with seemingly unlimited upsides. How does someone not only determine that the world is ready for affordable green energy but actually figure out a way to deliver it to the masses? How does someone see that there would be a demand for foreign exchange trading on Main Street and then actually make it accessible? I think we can all learn from this kind of boldness and daring, this kind of innovation and determination.

CLASH OF THE MENTORS

I'd like to share a mentor story with you that happened during my first year working in New York City at Shearson Lehman Hutton. In this case, one of my mentors gave me advice that conflicted with that of another one of my mentors—my dad—and I was caught in the middle.

A little background: The employee manual at Shearson Lehman clearly stated I was entitled to only two weeks of vacation and couldn't take any time off during the first six months. In addition, my manager had told me that because we were in the banking field and handled millions of dollars, we had to take two consecutive weeks off every year. Commonplace in most financial institutions, this rule ensures employees aren't embezzling or hiding anything. It's based on the theory that if an employee is away for two weeks, any embezzlement would somehow be revealed. I assumed I couldn't take even one day off because I needed to take two weeks together, so I was saving my money and waiting for summer.

For anyone working in the New York City financial markets at the time, Thursday was the big night out because if you stayed out late and were tired the next day, at least it was Friday. You'd deal with it and get through the day, knowing the weekend would provide reprieve.

One typical Thursday I went out for happy hour with the traders from my desk, and soon they started inviting me on a regular basis. Fortunately, I didn't have to worry about getting home because I had a car service at my disposal, courtesy of either my firm or the brokers entertaining us. Even so, I was always careful not to overindulge so I could be sharp the next day.

On one of those Thursday evenings, a mentor of mine who was also one of my bosses (and by the way, when you were a low-life clerk like me, everyone on the trading desk was your boss), told me I was a good, hard-working kid. After I thanked him for the kind words, I mentioned I hadn't had a day off in nine months. He looked at me like I was nuts because foreign exchange traders typically got four-plus weeks off. I explained that junior guys like me were subject to the "two weeks only" rule.

Letting me know those rules weren't followed to a tee, especially at the trading desk, he suggested I have a good time and call in "sick" the next day. In fact, he told me to call the night trading desk right away (this was 1988, so I had to find a pay phone) and leave a message for the chief dealer that I wouldn't be in the next day. "Just say you're not feeling that great and you need a day off," he said. "So drink up and have a good time, kid. Here's a car voucher for a limo home. See you Monday."

Wow! What a cool mentor! Here I was, barely 21, and I had full clearance to party all night, with free limo service home around 3 or 4 a.m. Then I could sleep until noon and enjoy a three-day weekend! I deserved it.

Well, thanks to my dad, it didn't work out that way.

I was still living at home and at that time, my father happened to work directly across the street from my office. He had to be in around 7:30 a.m., and normally I had to be in at 7:00 a.m., so he did me a major favor and drove in earlier so we could go together.

We had a sweet ride. The FBI let Dad drive cars they confiscated from convicted drug dealers, and at the time, he had a Peugeot sports car. The idea was that not many people would expect a fed to be driving such a unique car. This helped him remain incognito. Not only did we have a cool car, but we took the express bus lanes. We flew by the traffic and hardly ever got pulled over. If we did, Dad flashed his badge and we just kept going.

Our routine was to leave the house about 6:20 a.m., and we would comfortably get in by seven. When my dad was off for the week, I'd have to start out around 5:45 a.m. on a bus, so this carpool setup was a godsend.

This particular night, I finally stumbled in at my parents' house around 3:45 a.m. I had to get on the phone right away and cancel my credit cards because I couldn't find my wallet. Was it stolen? Did I leave it in the limo? After about 20 minutes of being on hold and cancelling my cards, I wrote a BIG note on my bedroom door: "Dad, do NOT wake me up. I called the night desk and told them I'm sick today. Thanks." I recall the satisfied smile on my face when I taped the note to my door. I figured I'd sleep for 10 hours then wake up and go to the mall for lunch—and it would be Friday, the beginning of a long weekend! All this with the blessing of one of my mentors at work… it was even his idea!

It felt like only five minutes after my head hit the pillow when my dad was standing over me. It was 5:45 a.m., and I heard, "Get in the shower—time to go to work."

Totally groggy with less than a couple hours of sleep, I was ticked off at first because I figured he missed my note and woke me up for no reason. The grand plan had struck a speed bump. But that's okay, I thought. I'll fall back asleep in a flash. "Dad, didn't you see the note? I called in sick. It's OK—one of my bosses gave me the day off."

He would have none of it. He explained to me that if you were out drinking and partying with people from work, you must show up the next day—and on time. No excuses.

"I know that, Dad, of course I know that, but this is different." I half explained, half pleaded. "My own boss suggested I stay out late and take the day off. I worked nine months without one day off, and I need a day off. He wants me to take it off."

It didn't matter what I said. He insisted I get dressed and show up on time. Ugh! I was a mess. I managed to shower okay but had a tough time shaving. Finally, in my suit and tie (no casual Fridays in 1988), I clambered into the Peugeot and slept all the way in. Next thing I knew, I was at my desk.

One of my colleagues who'd been with me most of the night but knew enough to slow down because of work the next day, was shocked. He couldn't believe I was sitting in front of him. He said, "Just three to four hours ago you could barely walk and now you're here? I thought you were sleeping in."

I told him I decided to come in anyway. He warned me, "Do not make any trades. Just hang out a few hours and ask to go home early." Now that was wise mentoring. And I did get to leave early.

Was I proud of myself and my behavior? Of course not. I did earn some warrior points for showing up which never would have happened if my dad hadn't forced me to go, but I certainly didn't fool anyone. Most of the trading desk knew I was basically useless, and quite frankly, I could have made a very costly error had I handled any important trades.

However, I did learn a few lessons from my dad. When you're making your way up the ladder, you can't fall for any traps. Even though one of my professional "mentors" told me to call in sick, it could have been a setup. Or maybe a test. Perhaps he just wanted to give me friendly "helpful" advice. But that doesn't mean it was sound advice. "Sean" was an excellent trader—calm under pressure and quite knowledgeable. However, he also had a drinking problem. His good career could have been a great career had he been more responsible with his nights out.

Your Takeaway

As you work on raising your personal equity, be sure to choose your mentors wisely, and be aware that no perfect mentors exist. Choose the best traits from the best people and combine and adopt them to make yourself better.

Obviously, my wisest choices here would have been to take the blue-collar work ethic of my dad and combine it with the calm trading demeanor and skills of my mentor from work. Of course at age 21, I was in the early stages of developing my PE and wasn't much concerned yet about my personal and professional development. I just wanted to make as much money as I could and go out and have a good time. However, the lesson made indelible by the misery of my hangover has stuck with me to this day.

One of the keys to thinking big is total focus. I think of it almost as a controlled neurosis, which is a quality I've noticed in many highly successful entrepreneurs.
—Donald Trump

CHAPTER 10

COUSIN VITO
HIGH PE PERSONIFIED

I'd like to share a success story with you about my second cousin Vito Denora, who is a mentor to many. I've literally seen his story unfold before my eyes throughout my life, and it's always inspired me. In addition, it's another great example of using the visioning principle and the Law of Attraction described in this book.

My research for this story "forced" me to take a trip to Italy to interview Vito, my mom's first cousin. Forced me? Well, not really. I don't ever need to be forced to skip off to Italy for three weeks with my wife and kids. Touring the world whenever you wish is one of the many perks of high Personal Equity so I hope you have a good set of luggage. I simply couldn't have finished this book without sitting down with cousin Vito. At least that's the story I told my accountant, and I'm stickin' to it.

ITALIAN IMMIGRANTS

My mother's maiden name is Claire Denora, but her family in Italy knows her as "Chiarina," affectionately meaning "little Chiara," or little Claire. Her father (my grandfather) was John Denora. His was the classic story of an immigrant coming to America to build a dream in the early 1900s on a boat to Ellis Island, New York. He arrived in this country in 1919 at the age of 18 with less than a dollar in his pocket. He moved in with his brother Francesco who had come a few years earlier, and stayed until he could get a job and a place of his own. He soon started his own business delivering ice in the summer and coal in the winter. Most of the Italians that came from Bari, Italy worked in this field. No one knows exactly how these Barese (people from Bari) were drawn to this specific field of work. They probably started out in it and hired friends and family when they saw the great demand for these services.

John then got married, had four children (the youngest, my mother Claire), and lived a respectable, fulfilling life. Never rich, never poor. A proud man who truly loved America and the opportunity it afforded him and his family.

Think about these Italian immigrants from 100 years ago. It must have been quite intimidating leaving a home where you were safe and secure. No one was starving because they always had plenty of food living in such a fertile farming region. They didn't have CNN, MTV, or the Internet showing off the American lifestyle and the "land of opportunity." The success stories all came by word of mouth across the Atlantic. These Italians were safe and secure in their own country but had little to no chance to ever get ahead in life. In addition, they could barely read or write Italian, never mind English. Yet they took the plunge.

Of course my grandfather's story was special to me, but his story was shared by millions. You'll find lots of these stories of people emigrating from all parts of Europe back in the early 20th century. Even today, people want to get into the United States and make a better life for themselves and their families. I wonder: What do these people murmur under their breath when they hear about someone born in the U.S. with a decent education who's still struggling to make ends meet?

COUSIN VITO

Back to Vito Denora. He was my grandfather's nephew, son of his brother Pasquale Denora, who never made the journey to America. Pasquale was happy remaining in Italy and lived a good long life there. I knew some of the details of Vito's success, but it wasn't until my "formal interview" with him during the summer of 2011 that I got the real story. It felt a bit strange interviewing my 76-year-old cousin who's known me all my life. He came to America in the late 1950s, when he was in his early 20s, and moved in with my grandfather until he could get on his feet like my grandfather had done with a family member back in 1919.

Vito was (and still is) a short, stout, and powerfully built man who would promise anyone who hired him that he would do the work of two men. He was always trying to show his value. He told me more than a few times that whenever he saw two men loading bags of cement sand, he would insist on lifting the bags all by himself. To use his term, he worked like a "jackass." Every time he used that term, I had to chuckle. I think something was lost or added in the translation. I think he meant to say "mule" as in a hardworking animal that did all the heavy lifting. However, "jackass" has a charm to it as well in this story as it hints to that burning feeling inside that he was better than that. He knew he had more in store for his immediate future, but he had to pay his dues. He planned to leave the grunt work to the people with no dreams.

So here was Vito, age 24, a basic laborer who didn't speak English, who knew deep down he was born for a better life. Vito's story is inspiring because although he wasn't very educated, he had a great understanding of what he needed to do to become successful. He surely hadn't read any of Napoleon Hill's work, and Anthony Robbins wasn't even born yet. Where was his drive coming from? What skills did he have to organize his plan and follow through? It had to be innate. His own father opted to stay in Italy and pass up on the land of opportunity, yet some of his brothers and his son couldn't resist.

"...Life, Liberty and the Pursuit of Happiness." For most Americans, these are just words they had to remember for a grade-school history test. For others, they call forth a passion; a mission, a calling that has to be fulfilled. I often think about the major advantage my friends and I had growing up. Just about everyone at least graduated high school and was somewhat literate, and yet now so many are unemployed, in debt, or bankrupt. I often think about how I would be doing if I were in a similar situation as Vito's today. What if I were plopped into a city in the middle of China? How well would I do? China is a great example of a booming economy with a huge economic future similar to that of the U.S. in the early 20th century. Think about the hurdles and the challenges. A new language, new rules, no contacts... yet millionaires are being created every day in China. The opportunity is limitless. It makes you think about what we have here in the U.S. If you're reading this book in English right now, you already have a big advantage over my cousin Vito in 1958.

IT ALL STARTS WITH A PLAN AND GOALS

So how did Vito's story play out? He had a plan and goals. Every success story starts with a plan. But did he write down his goals the way you and I do? Did he have specific written goals with timelines and dates? Short-term and long-term goals taped to his mirror where he could see them every morning when he was shaving? You know... the stuff we've been hearing all our lives... the strategies that have been proven to work so well? No. He didn't even know there was a science to becoming successful. But he had something perhaps even more powerful than written goals; he had a clear, obsessive vision of what he wanted and where he wanted to be. This steady vision pulsated in his mind constantly as he labored nine to ten hours a day digging ditches or laying brick in all types of weather. While he was driving to work, he wasn't thinking about checking his email or how his sports team did last night; he wasn't looking forward to attending the cocktail party this weekend or playing around on Facebook. He wasn't dreaming of buying a new car or taking a vacation he couldn't afford. No. He was thinking of where he wanted to be and what he had to do in that moment to get closer to his goal of owning his own business and having people work for *him.*

Think about the advantage you have by simply reading this book and the other countless books that have cracked the code as to what makes people successful. Think of how exhausting it must have been for Vito to persevere without knowing any of the success techniques such as *simply writing your goals down.* I'm not advising you to become obsessive with your goals like Vito. He had to obsess about his goals because that's all he knew. For you and me it can be easier.

In fact, right now, write your goals down; then going forward, review them two to three times a day. Is that so hard? Will you do it? Why not do it right now? Put the book down and write some goals for the next three days, three weeks, three months. Keep them in your pocket and read them two to three times a day. Try it. Is this the first time you've gotten this advice? Probably not. The main reason you wouldn't stop right now and write down a few goals, or at least read the goals you do have handy, is you don't really believe it works. If you knew with certainty, like I do, you would be writing in the margins right now. Go for it.

HEADING FOR LEADERSHIP

With a look to the future, Vito became laser focused on his boss. Vito wanted to own and run his own business just like him, but even better. That was his big goal—so he studied his boss.

"What makes this boss so special? Why do I have to get dirty and sweaty every day and he doesn't? Why does he get to drive a nice new air conditioned truck from job to job and never break a sweat? Why does he get to decide who works today and who goes home? Why does he get to decide how much profit margin to build in on his price quotes? How did he get into a position to have 12 thankful "jackasses" working for him?"

This is what Vito was thinking, not in a vindictive way, but in a healthy, positive way. He wasn't jealous so much as he was in awe. He wanted to be like his boss, but even better. He wanted to treat his employees better than his boss was treating him and his co-workers; he wanted to pay them more; he wanted to use higher quality materials and create "masterpieces" and have word get out that the best mason in town had finally arrived.

These were some of his short-term goals, the fastest way to secure a financial future for him and his family. Could Vito have gone back to school? Could he have learned English, received his Government Equivalency Diploma (GED), enrolled in a local community college, gotten straight A's, and transferred into a prestigious academic institution? Maybe... *or he could just work on his Personal Equity.* He decided to run with what he knew best. Simply learn from those around him, always work hard, always be supportive and helpful, always show up on time, do what he said he was going to do every time. Be trustworthy and reliable, and become a leader, a magnet that attracts other quality people in his laborers' world. These are some of the main ingredients of Personal Equity.

As a result of his rising PE, Vito soon started getting a few of his own projects on weekends and at night. His PE enabled him to recruit co-workers to follow him and work for him for extra pay. They trusted him. Vito was emerging as a leader, as a potential new boss for people who admired him. Oftentimes guys would branch out and never finish projects or run out of money and not pay their staff. This was pretty common. So working an extra five hours a night for someone new was viewed as risky—but Vito's PE erased those concerns.

This was new territory for him, but he acted the part and kept forging ahead. The visions he'd been focusing on so clearly were becoming a reality. Was he excited? Was he surprised? Not really. Everything was going according to plan. If you truly believe in your goals and your destiny, you'll find that you don't get excited when you arrive because it feels normal. You *expected* it. This is a good thing. It means you're growing.

I recall being 17 years old and driving to the mall for the first time all by myself. I was very tentative and so happy when I pulled into the parking lot successfully. Today? We all fully expect to arrive at our driving destination unscathed. In fact, if we hit any kind of traffic or if someone cuts us off, we get angry. Getting there on time and parking the car are givens. If we leave on time, we don't consider any other result. In fact, we may have been chatting on our hands-free phone or listening to a favorite song and don't even remember the driving experience.

How odd would it seem if someone congratulated us for arriving safely and on time for every errand we ran each day? This is a great example of how we stretch ourselves and make what may seem extraordinary to a brand new driver seem quite ordinary for you and me.

Okay—back to Vito Denora. It wasn't long before Vito had a thriving business all to himself. All he did was deliver exactly as promised and a little more, whereas his competition always seemed to be late and sloppy.

Vito is all about building a team and taking people along for the ride. As he was one of nine siblings, he sent for a few of his brothers from Italy to help him. But he didn't play favorites. Some of his brothers were hard workers and some were just okay, and Vito had no problem promoting a stranger over a brother if he earned it.

CITTÀ DEL PANE

One day Vito's brother Michael approached him with another opportunity. He wanted Vito to check out his business plan and perhaps partner with him to buy a fledging little bakery in Union City, New Jersey. His brother wanted to convert it to a commercial bakery, specifically to bake bread for local stores and restaurants. This was only a few short years after Vito had arrived in America and he'd achieved all his goals: he had a crew working for him, he had a new truck, and he didn't have to get sweaty and dirty—although he still did from time to time to show what hard work is all about. He'd gone from "jackass" to boss. Mission accomplished, yes? Vito had just turned the corner in the masonry/construction business. With sky high PE in his business world, he had too much work to handle as it was, and he was making more money than he'd planned. He didn't need to start a bakery! He could live a comfortable life and be yet another nice success story. But not Vito. He realized he had a gift of some sort, and he had a large extended family. He wanted to bring more people up with him.

The town that Vito and my grandfather come from is called Altamura, also known as "Città del Pane," or "City of Bread." In fact, you'll see signs on the highway as you enter town bragging about the town's famous bread. Altamura is a small, ancient town, about a 30-minute drive west of the port town of Bari on the southeast part of the boot-shaped peninsula. Ask any Italian where the best bread comes from, and the answer is always "Altamura." Just as you could ask any American where the best potatoes or crab cakes come from and the answers would be Idaho and Maryland, respectively.

So Vito's brother Michael suggested that the New York/New Jersey market had a need for the world's greatest bread. Part of the idea came from the simple fact that he was homesick for a decent loaf himself! In addition, numerous owners of fine Italian restaurants knew good bread when they tasted it and would surely try a product baked by natives of the legendary Altamura. Therefore, the plan was to somehow re-create the same Altamura-type bread and build another successful business. Vito knew this would diversify his income and give him even more leverage. Plus, the oven would do a lot of the work for him!

Now Vito had come from the bread capital of Europe, but he'd never baked a loaf in his life. He didn't have any bakery knowledge, but that doesn't matter when you have a surging PE quotient. His PE would easily qualify him to obtain a loan for the brick ovens, hire quality people, and get commercial accounts to buy his bread. Ah, the benefits of high Personal Equity. He could do whatever he set his mind to do. Vito agreed to start the bakery business with his brother Michael because he saw *an opportunity to bake loaves of bread for pennies and sell them for dollars*—while still managing his thriving construction business. In addition, this was a way to have some of his family and friends ride his PE wave. You see, people with high PE aren't selfish—rather just the opposite. They know that taking advantage of others or stomping on people to get ahead is a fool's game, whereas bringing people up with them spreads the wealth and helps the whole community.

"I WANNA BE BIG!"

This is what Vito was saying to himself when he started the bakery business. When he told me this line in his broken English, I had to try not to laugh. Here was a guy about one foot shorter than I am getting all emotional about his desire to be BIG. Of course I knew exactly what he meant. He wanted to build a big business, not grow a foot taller and the intensity of his desire to grow helped him achieve his goal.

MY VIEW ON THE MATTER OF GOALS

> *"Dream Big, like when you were small. Know your destination and enjoy the journey."*
> —*Brenden Kenny*

If I had been his personal coach back in those early days and known what I know now, I would've sat him down and had him write out his goals. By what date would he be open? How many sales would he like his first month… first six months? Where would he like to be in a year? But again, he had all this in his head and was living and breathing it 24/7. He didn't need goals on paper to remind him.

So what technique works best for us to achieve our goals? Do we write down our goals or do we live them every moment of every day like Vito? In my opinion, writing our goals down on paper is more efficient and helps us live a more relaxed and successful life. Why? Because our modern lives tend to be more complicated and distracted than my cousin's was back then. Writing down our goals and reading them daily helps impress them on our subconscious mind so our mind will continue to work on them even when we're not consciously focusing on them. That said, somewhere in the middle is where we want to be. We need some kind of emotional intensity behind our goals or we won't have the motivation to achieve them.

Think about a goal you really wanted to achieve. You probably wrote it down and obsessed about it a lot. That's what kids do. I see this with my 13-year-old daughter Stephanie. She wanted an Apple computer. We told her if she got good grades and did a few other things, we'd give it to her for her eighth-grade graduation. She had a photo of the computer cut out and taped on her mirror, and she would talk about it every day. She'd stare at it on the Internet and show me its features on the website. She was rather obsessive about it… and she tends to get what she wants. I didn't teach her this. Kids know it works.

As adults, we're often too rational and pragmatic. We need to balance our pragmatism with a dose of Stephanie's obsession and Cousin Vito's Italian intensity.

BACK TO ITALIA

So what happened with Vito and the bakery? Well, the bakery did become big. It sold bread and then gourmet packaged cookies to all the fine restaurants and delicatessens throughout the New York metro area. Vito's next plan was to return home to Altamura with $500,000 in cash. This was a small fortune back in the late 1960s when you could buy a fine four-bedroom home for $30,000. He mentioned this goal to one of his American cousins and she laughed. That was a crazy amount of money to her.

Why back to Italy? Wasn't America the land of opportunity? Vito left southern Italy because the economy had become stagnant and there wasn't much demand for his work. Now he had a wildly successful bakery and all the finer things in life in the great U.S. of A. He also had four daughters who were all American citizens. Why sell? Why leave?

Having recently returned from Italy myself, I can see why people might like to live there—especially if you're living in your hometown. The weather, the food, the people, the "dolce vita" lifestyle—all good. So Vito returned to his hometown of Altamura after 15 years in the States with a lot more than the $500K he'd planned on taking. In fact, he returned a legitimate millionaire in the 1970s, with all his newly developed talent and skyrocketing PE. His journey that took him from digging ditches to millionaire in 15 years was worth more than any Ivy League MBA.

"Create a community, inspire a movement"
—*Charles Costello*

Taking his sleepy town by storm, Vito quickly bought land and built apartment and condo complexes. Leveraging his money and his reputation to build an even greater empire, he hired hundreds of people and built much-needed affordable housing. He'd learned a lot about how business works by being an entrepreneur and lit up his hometown, showing the not-so-motivated townspeople how to make things happen for them. He became a true leader and an inspiration for Altamura, Italy, which today is a thriving and charming metropolis.

Vito is now 76 years old and looks 10–15 years younger. He appears fit and relaxed. He loved taking me and my family around and pointing out which buildings he'd built, and is still building today, and showing us which cranes soaring in the sky were his. He then took us out to the finest restaurants with his entire extended family.

He was very proud to hear I was doing so well and was working on writing a book about success. You should've seen the delighted look on his face when I told him I was dedicating a chapter to his story.

So what's the bottom line here? If a barely educated laborer from another country with no formal sales skills or training can live out his dream, *why can't we all?*

Do not dwell in the past, do not dream of the future,
concentrate the mind on the present moment.
—*Buddha*

EPILOGUE

FLOWERS AND DIAMONDS

Have you ever wondered why we are here? Why our human race exists in the first place and why we're the only species that can think and have unique thoughts? I believe our mission on this planet is to reach a higher level—that all species are here to grow and evolve, to become better. Hopefully, we can live to an old age and have more happiness than sadness. However, living a long life isn't our most important aim. Rather, I believe our true mission is to grow and evolve every day, no matter how many days or years we have. To become a positive force… to achieve enlightenment and be present in the moment.

Sadly, most people on this planet aren't aware of this mission, and those who have a glimpse of it, like me and, I hope, you—know how difficult it is. It's a struggle every second of every day to not let our negative thoughts consume us and our emotions distract us. To not let silly things upset us or petty arguments with our spouse or friends blow up into something completely destructive. To simply forgive and to look at the bright side… which brings me to flowers and diamonds.

Why are we as a human race so attracted to flowers and diamonds? You may be thinking, "Well, Joe, flowers are pretty and smell nice, so naturally we're attracted to them." But I think there's a deeper reason.

Billions of years ago, the earth was covered with basic green vegetation. Just green leaves, vines, and trees. No flowers… not yet. These green organisms were the beginnings of all plant life as we know it. Then, a few plants started to evolve and actually produce flowers. These plants were the first to break through and become "enlightened"—to better themselves, to bloom and add beauty to the world, to attract honeybees and birds.

Why do humans stop and adore a beautiful flower? Because at a deep level, we yearn to be like that flower. *A flowering plant has massive PE!* This is why we give flowers to either celebrate or cheer people up.

You've probably heard the advice to "stop and smell the roses." That's great advice! People who are too busy to "stop and smell the roses" are lost. They're not happy; they're caught up in the rat race of life. Those who do stop, admire, and smell the fragrance of flowers are more grounded and connected to the journey, and usually happier. For that moment, as they take that deep breath, nothing else matters. They are present.

Diamonds also attract our attention. Created from basic organic coal that's been under extreme pressure for eons, they're beautiful, sparkling with light, and incredibly strong. Evolving under unique conditions, they've become truly enlightened gems. *Like flowers, diamonds have astronomical PE.*

Flowers and diamonds are admired by every culture on the planet. As humans, we can't help but adore them because they're symbols of enlightenment and proof that we were put here to follow the same path.

The idea of developing and nurturing your PE goes hand-in-hand with this theory. If your PE is high, you will naturally attract all kinds of people who are on the same path. Good people, people who are grounded, ethical, and have some idea, either consciously or unconsciously, of why we are here. The very same people who often "stop and smell the roses" will appear in your life—whether socially or for business.

IN CLOSING

If you take to heart the many stories and ideas I share in this book, you will become as attractive as a flower or diamond to others on the same journey. You'll become a magnet everyone will be attracted to, but only a few will be able to explain why. Consciously

> *There are only two mistakes one can make along the road to truth; not going all the way, and not starting.*
> —*Buddha*

develop your Personal Equity in every moment. Improve your listening skills, learn to use the universal laws of manifestation, strengthen your connection with others, give before you get, increase your integrity, and emulate others you admire. Then you will experience greatness in whatever you pursue.

I don't agree with the phrase "beyond your wildest dreams." If you've read this far, you know I don't believe anything could happen "beyond your dreams." You need to dream it first! My final advice? Dream big and follow through, then watch your dream-story come to life.

MEET JOE O.,
MR. PERSONAL EQUITY

For Joe Occhiogrosso—please, call him Joe O.—success comes down to power, but not the kind of power you might expect from a man whose background and career are the stuff of business legend.

He certainly has the resume of a power player: Joe graduated Rutgers University with degrees in Economics and Philosophy at the age 20. He won the "Mr. Rutgers" bodybuilding title a year earlier followed by a ten-year wild ride on Wall Street trading in the 24 hour global currency markets for major banks. He then started his entrepreneurial career by shifting into the nascent Professional Employer Organization (PEO) industry. He co-founded Compensation Solutions, a $150 million-a-year provider of Fortune 500-level HR services to small and mid-sized companies. Already a great career for anyone, but by then, in 2003, Joe O. was not yet 40 years old.

Time for another shift: In 2003, Joe sold his interest in the PEO to a group of private investors to start All-Pro Title Agency. Always looking for a competitive edge, he combined high-tech paperless efficiency with his now-famous networking skills to double revenue each year under his guidance.

Partnering with All-Pro co-founders Frank Marone and three-time Super Bowl Champion Bart Oates, Esq., however, revealed the true source of Joe's success and networking skills, and helped define what makes his approach unique as he diversified on to other successful ventures. He's captured that energy in his new book: *The Power of Personal Equity: Simple Steps to Recession-Proof Your Business or Career.*

The concept of Personal Equity has far-reaching consequences for the success of any entrepreneur or businessperson, yet it's not about money. It's not about your portfolio, your education, your reputation or any tangible item you could buy or sell. For Joe O., Personal Equity (PE) is the result of an ongoing drive toward personal and professional enlightenment, and it begins and ends with others. It's a measurement of how well you combine principles and standards with business savvy and wealth. And at the end of the day, it's not about rising above others or leaving them in your wake; it's about how many people you take along with you.

Of course, this philosophy is a perfect fit for any corporate executive, salesperson or aspiring entrepreneur. It's particularly helpful for a career in direct selling—a career that Joe never before considered until recently. In less than 18 months in direct selling, Joe has already created a residual income in excess of $150k a month and growing. He is already considered one of the most successful direct selling professionals in the world. However, this book extends to anyone in business. And that's the power-secret of Joe's success. Ride your vision, give before you get, invest in yourself and others, and learn how to network. There may be no guarantees in a turbulent economy, but Joe O.'s concept of Personal Equity is a badly needed framework for recession-proofing your hard work and growing your business. Joe has already shared his proven concepts with 10's of thousands and has now created an easy-to-read book sharing it all.

Joe resides in northern New Jersey and is happily married to Annmarie Occhiogrosso. Together they are proud parents to 3 children: Alex 16, Stephanie 14 and Frankie 10. Joe enjoys spending time with family, playing baseball and volunteering time and raising awareness for the Interfaith Food Pantry, one of his favorite charities.

MENTOR LIST

Joe O's personal list of high PE people to thank for their friendship and inspiration. To borrow a phrase from the legendary Yogi Berra. "I'd like to thank these people for making this book necessary."

Michael Marotte, Esq.

I first met Mike in 1979 when I was a 13 year old Freshman at Monsignor Farrell High School in Staten Island, NY. We've been very close friends ever since. Mike is one of the top partners at the 100 year old law firm of Schenck, Price, Smith & King in Florham Park, NJ. He started out his career with a degree in chemical engineering and then he decided to go to law school after a few years. Mike started out his legal career with no clients and no real contacts and today is a million dollar producer. How did he achieve such success in such an overly competitive field? How does he have corporate and private clients flocking to him while making time for his lovely family and keeping his commitment to health and fitness? Duh . . . there answer is obvious . . . he has Joe O. as a friend guiding him along the way! That's not completely true. Mike is a brilliant lawyer with great skills. He is perhaps the best lawyer in the Northeast. I do know he does give me some credit for showing him how to slow down and have more fun. Too much work and no play makes Mike a dull boy. And I don't hang out with dull friends.

Mike has great Personal Equity as he has evolved into a master networker. The truth is he serves as a mentor to me. While most attorneys are always looking to bill every moment they spend working for a client, Mike is very generous with his time. He understands the "give before you get" rule and uses it to serve him well. We kind of evolved our Personal Equity together over the years before I even coined the phrase. We meet on a regular basis for lunch to discuss in detail what works and doesn't work as we grow our respective businesses. Mike and his wife Michelle were blessed a few years ago with a beautiful baby boy. I'm proud to be the godfather of his son. His name is Joseph – coincidence?

Frank Marone

Frank is another all-star PE person. I've known Frank for over 20 years and he is a natural at networking. His down-to-earth friendly persona serves as a magnet. Frank was a Vice President and senior foreign exchange currency broker at Noonan, Astley and Pearce when I joined his team back in 1990. He had a stellar reputation as being one of the highest paid and most respected brokers in NYC at the time. He rose to this great fame and fortune by simply being himself. Always telling the truth, always delivering what he said he would deliver and then some. Frank not only has great business instincts and street smarts but is fun to be around. He has a great ability to never take himself too seriously. I left Wall Street back in 1996, and when I was looking to team up with someone to start All-Pro Title Agency in 2003 Frank was one of the first people I called. I convinced him to leave the Wall Street world. I was honored to have Frank Marone join me. We have been working together as small business owners since 2003 and dove into the network marketing business together. Viridian Energy has changed both of our lives forever - both financially and spiritually. We are so much more conscious of the environment and how important that is for all of us. People will do more for a cause than they will ever do for money. Frank and I are convinced now more than ever that the more people you help the more money you will make. It's not just a clever phrase that sounds honorable. Frank and I know it to be a fact. I'm truly blessed to have Frank and his wife Susan as friends of mine. They live in the town next to me and they have an awesome backyard with a pool.

Bob Quintana

I have known Bob for more than 25 years. Bob is a great leader in the Network Marketing industry. He is a great friend that inspires me to always keep working on improving my game. His concept of combining your "skill set and mind set with execution" to achieve peak performance is something I work on every day. Bob brings great credibility and honor to what he likes to call the "relationship marketing" business. He never exaggerates or stretches the truth when sharing his experiences. He always tells it like it is. He is a tireless worker that focuses on helping others get what they want in life. Bob Quintana was one of my first real mentors and will always be a mentor of mine. It wasn't easy finding someone that likes to talk more than me – but I thank Bob for ending my search. He and his lovely wife Pennie enjoy a great life together and Annmarie and I love to spend time with them.

RECOMMENDED AUTHORS

Any and all books written by

Napoleon Hill

Dr. Bill Quain

Eckhart Tolle

Anthony Robbins

Robert Kiyosaki

Dan Millman

Patrick Snow

Quick Order & Information Request Form

Mentor Equity Press International
4809 Avenue N Suite 405, Brooklyn, NY 11234
Office: (718) 513-4648   Fax: (866) 583-7181

My name is:_____

Mailing Address:_____

City/State/Zip: _____

Telephone#: (Day)_____ (Evening) _____

I am interested in learning more about:

a._____ Seminars and Workshops for my church, group, or company.

b._____ Requesting Joe O to speak at my next event.

c._____ DVD's, CD's, or other products by Joe O.

d._____ Writing, publishing, or promoting my book or business.

e._____ Arranging a book signing fundraiser with Joe O.

f_____ My interest is not addressed above and I describe it below:

To receive Joe O's *Power of Personal Equity e-Newletter* please visit *www. JoeOBook.com* and enter your name and email address. This Newsletter is published periodically, filled with inspiring quotes, success strategies, and other information.

Quick Order Form

To order additional copies of this book call (718) 513-4648,
toll free (866) 583-7181 or email at *orders@MentorEquityPress.com*

Note: Quantity discounts available.

I would like to order _____ copies of *The Power of Personal Equity* at $19.95/book. *A portion of all book sales support charity, including Interfaith Food Pantry.*

Sales Tax: NY residents (only) add 8.875%   _____

Shipping & Handling: Add $5.65 per book.   _____

Free Audio CD with every purchase ($9.95 value) _____

Total Amount Enclosed (check or money order) _____

Make check payable to **Success Connection Team, Corp.**

Make a copy of this page, fill it out, mail or fax to above address.

www.ThePowerOfPersonalEquity.com

Quick Order Form Wholesale Prices

To purchase

The Power Of Personal Equity:
Simple Steps to Recession-Proof Your Business or Career
by Joe Occhiogrosso

PURCHASE VOLUME DISCOUNT WHOLESALE RATES

1-4 books: $19.95 each, plus *s/h

5-10 books: -10% discount $17.96 each, plus *s/h

11-25 books: -15% discount $16.96 each, plus *s/h

26-50 books: -20% discount $15.96 each, plus *s/h

51-100 books: -25% discount $14.96 each, plus *s/h

101-200 books: -30% discount $13.96 each, plus *s/h

201-500 books: -35% discount $12.96 each, plus *s/h

501+ books: Call 1-718-513-4648 or Toll-Free: 1-866-583-7181

Pricing is based on number of books ordered at one time, and paid-in-full

at time of ordering.

*s/h = Actual Shipping Cost plus $5.00 per order for handling.

Orders may be placed directly with publisher Mentor Equity Press by calling:
1-718-513-4648, email orders@MentorEquityPress.com or online at
www.MentorEquityPress.com

Prices as of September 2011 (Subject to change without notice).